ANNA BACHMEYER

STAND IN THE
Knowing

SQUARE TREE PUBLISHING

www.SquareTreePublishing.com

For more information about bulk purchases, please contact Square Tree Publishing at info@squaretreepublishing.com

Cover design by Sharon Marta.

ISBN 978-1-957293-31-8

DEDICATION

I dedicate this book to my grandma. She has been there for me in ways only eternity understands the impact of. Championing me with each step, listening as I process, and challenging me when needed. There truly is nothing hidden between us. She has seen the good, the hard, and the devastating, and she has loved me through it all. The facet of Jesus she reflects has been one that makes me feel seen and heard, and that has been priceless. I love you, and I am so honored and blessed to be your granddaughter.

Reviews

"For millennials raised in the church and done with religion, the Gen-Zers not content with the status quo and ready for mentorship; for those alone searching for community and depth, and for all who are curious of what a life of faith could look like, Anna Bachmeyer will take you by the hand and walk with you out of the mire of religion, through toxic thinking, and into a spacious place in her book, *Stand in the Knowing*.

Anna is as vulnerable as it gets, sharing experiences and an inside view of the process so many of us have gone through to find how to truly walk the Holy Spirit-led life — the divine dance — full of abundance. Along the way, you might even catch her enthusiasm for worship.

Her book is an excellent "no frills" look at all things kingdom living, the paradigm outside of what we've been taught in the four walls of the church. As she shares her journey, you'll find many of her stories are yours, helping you understand difficult seasons in your life. And as you do, you'll find freedom and reassurance in your steps."

Katherine Penniman
Founder of The Beholding Project

Reviews

"From the start, Anna Bachmeyer's book feels like a ' "pull-up-your-chair-and-make-a-cup-of-tea-so-that-we-can-have-a-heart-to-heart-together'," chat, giving us the gift of an unfiltered inside look at the journey and process God has taken her on, to enable her to understand her purpose as a daughter of God, to heal her broken places, and reveal her value and worth.

Anna's honesty is refreshing and provoking in all the right ways, providing a mirror for the reader as an invitation to explore their own walk with God. There is something so profound about listening to someone else's lived experience and discovering you're not alone, and that there is a way through your current circumstances towards greater hope and the future God has in mind for you.

If you have struggled with self-worth, insecurities, fear, excuses, shame, guilt, feeling broken and a bit all over the place, you'll find a home for your heart in *Stand in the Knowing*. This book gives the reader hope and permission to bring their beautiful mess and cloudy confusion before a kind, gracious, and loving Father who knows how to lead his children into healing and freedom."

Louise Campion, singer-songwriter, producer, and independent music artist coach
London, United Kingdom

TABLE OF CONTENTS

Introduction

THE KINGDOM'S INSIDE OF YOU

"There is a kingdom inside of you, and you have authority over more than you know," he spoke as he prophesied over me. He described Elsa, from the movie *Frozen*, who had left her kingdom and went into the mountains to create her own ice kingdom.

What did that mean, there is a kingdom inside of me? It left me with so many questions. I didn't really understand what God was saying at the time, so I shelved this word. Then, when I had entered a season in my life where all had been stripped away, leaving just me and the Lord, I sat down at the piano and started singing, "There's a kingdom inside of me, there's a kingdom that I can't yet see; there's a kingdom inside of me, there's a kingdom that I don't fully see. Maybe I can't see it—maybe I just don't believe it—maybe I don't want to see it; or maybe I just fear it." Was this Biblical? I didn't know. That following Sunday at church, the pastor read this verse: "The kingdom realm of God does not come simply by obeying principles or by waiting for signs. The kingdom is not discovered in one place or another, for the kingdom realm of God is already expanding within some of you" (Luke 17:21).

There it was. The verse I needed to anchor this search deep within me. I did not know what I was looking for or what it would look like, but I needed to know more. Was this kingdom a sign, anointing, or maybe a gift? What **was** this kingdom I was looking for? How come I couldn't see it? I wanted to see it, I wanted to believe in it, but there was this frustration inside of me, gnawing at me. It seemed as if I was chasing the wind. I was looking for it in signs and proof of this Christian life I was walking in. What I didn't realize was the kingdom was *Him*. I was chasing after *Him*. I wanted God to come alive within me; I wanted to be awakened to Him. He was the proof I had been looking for within myself. To see fruit that He was walking with me, and I with Him.

It amazes me how the Lord can give a prophetic word or picture (or, in my case, a prophetic song) of where He wants to take us. Even with the words written in front of my face, I still could not see or understand the meaning and significance of what He was saying to me. It was His strategic way, having me write a song He knew I would sing, like a prayer, so that I may see my heart's desire to know Him more and sing it into existence.

This has been my journey. Finding answers to what my spirit always knew was alive and inside me. It is the memories, thoughts, and meditations and what I've learned through them. It is the song I sing over and over and over myself. And, may I say, it has been a wild ride.

What does it look like to believe that the Great I Am chooses to do life in and with you and me? What does it look like to believe every word He has ever spoken; every yes and amen, and every promise given? What does it feel like to know you are who He says you are (because to deny it would be to deny your very being)? What does it look like to choose to believe His reality over what you see as reality in your life? To live in His truth and trust Him with every step you take?

This is where I am, where I am going, and where my journey began. This is my hope—that God would speak to you about who you are, who He is, and give you breakthrough to go deeper in ways you have only imagined through the simplicity of knowing Him and letting Him know you. Friend, I ask that you lean into, and stand in the knowing of who you are by believing His reality over you.

Chapter 1

EMBRACING THE PROCESS

"Character is the leadership quality developed through the tough stuff of life experience, which empowers you to take the God-given talent in you to its highest potential. Whatever lesson you are learning right now is part of that journey." —Jamie Galloway[1]

I remember sitting on the couch, laughing so hard I could barely breathe. My husband had said something that hit my funny bone. I was caught off guard as tears rushed in, breaking through the laughter that was masking the pain within. I had been in a season of such negativity and seriousness that to laugh was good for my soul, but what I needed most was to grieve the season that preceded it.

My husband and I had left a church we had poured all our energy into for four years and where we had grown in leaps and bounds. We were young with passion, fire, and energy, but toward the end of our time there, things went sour fast. What we had thought was a family was more of a transaction. When concerns and needs came up, we were met with manipulation and betrayal. We tried our best to walk out all this in peace,

---

[1] *Jamie Galloway, Author and founder of Jamie Galloway Ministries*

unscathed—but there were casualties in saying goodbye. We were two of them. To add to all this, our little family of three was about to become a family of four in just a few months. Two big transitions in our lives didn't leave much time to process our emotions and the closure we so desperately wanted. To be honest, I wasn't sure I knew *how* to feel, let alone *what* I was feeling. Although I had gone through some healing from past hurts before, I didn't realize the magnitude of this trauma until years later.

I struggled so much with the stillness. I was no longer busy doing weekly worship, prayer room nights, youth group, or Sunday worship services. It was just me and my two little boys now. I was done with this; I just wanted to heal what needed to be healed and move onto the next season. You know, time to wipe away the tears, pull up my britches, and keep on trucking. "I'm strong; this doesn't hurt, this is just a bump in my life," I would tell myself. "Stop being so emotional about it, geez!" Yet most days I would just cry. I'd listened to worship music to drown it all out. At least God's presence gave me a reason to be emotional, so it had some place to come out. Apparently being caught crying because I was grieving or hurt just wasn't okay in my mind. Pushing my feelings down and keeping everything to myself was the norm. But deep within my heart, I grieved. Everything I thought God was going to do suddenly vanished, and my dreams seemed so far away.

Things only grew harder as the devil would tell me, "The church you just left will do the very things you dreamed you'd be a part of, but now you won't be there." I felt empty, like a bystander looking from the outside while others moved forward. My whole identity was wrapped in the prophetic words of a group of people I was no longer connected to. I thought my heart was yearning for the things of God, but maybe I was more desperate to be someone God was proud of.

The grieving was happening, whether I liked it or not, and the healing process was painfully slow. I was so used to *doing*—jumping to the next thing, being involved, being part of the next conference—that the stillness was brutal. I thought if I could pass the test faster, I would get myself out of this process that was taking way longer than I thought it should. So I absorbed all I could by listening to teachings and reading books. What I didn't know was it would be the beginning of a seven-year wilderness experience.

Embracing the Process

One night during a visit with my mom, I walked into the computer room where she was so I could talk with her. She was listening to a teaching, and I came in at just the right moment. The man who was speaking said something that jumped off the screen and slapped me in the face: **"If you don't embrace your process, God will close the womb of your promise."**

It hit me like a ton of bricks. In that moment I realized I was stiff-arming God's process for me. Sitting with my thoughts as they ran through my head like a hamster on a wheel going nowhere was brutal. I was resisting being still and simply enjoying being with the Lord.

I was rushing through this precious time with Him, scrambling to get back to what I thought was normal. I couldn't see that He wanted this time with me to strengthen my roots in Him, to allow me to be nurtured by Him, in all those places in me that hurt so deeply. It was about refocusing and coming back to God as my audience of one. In retrospect, my life got wrecked, in a good way, by everything He was showing me. He tore down strongholds and lies I believed about Him and myself. I say now of that season, "If for not all that, I don't know where my relationship with the Lord would be today."

Whenever God is doing something in our lives, He always brings us through a process. Many people talk about the promises of walking with God, but not many talk about the process. I know the process can be hard, it can be slow, and even feel like death itself. This is why we avoid it. Who enjoys subjecting themselves to pain on purpose? The pain of letting go, facing our fears, or even walking in healing? Because of this, the process has been turned into an obstacle we want to jump over or go around; a hurdle we desperately try to get out of or avoid having to go through or cut corners on to make it to the other side faster. But there is no shortcut when building character or healing pain. There are no corners to cut when building a relationship with the Lord, in creating trust, or when He is refining us. We can expect the same when God gives us a promise. It's what we hold onto during the process, not a promise to avoid going through one.

Let's take a closer look at the word "process" and break it down.

Process
1. A series of actions or steps taken in order to achieve a particular end.
2. The Latin origin is <u>progression</u>.

Progression
1. The process of developing or moving gradually toward a more advanced state.
2. A passage or movement from one note or chord to another.[2]

The process is simply putting one foot in front of the other. It's a continual motion of moving forward. As a musician, I love to define it this way: without the movement (or change) of each note or chord, there is no melody or song to hear. Each step is like a note of our life being played. To hear the full melody with all its intricate details, crescendos, and soft intimate sounds, we have to play each note in order, the way it is written. If not, a different melody, or just noise, is created, like the clanging of a gong.

The process is meant to flow; to be a beautiful dance between you and the King of Kings, drawing you closer into His loving arms as you gaze into the eyes of love. Time has no limits there, for His grace empowers you to do what is in front of you. It is a dance where we put our feet upon His feet, our hands in His, like a little girl dancing with her father.

The process is where our foundation is built and where our roots grow deep. In the Old Testament, as the Israelites left Egypt, they followed God's cloud by day and His fire by night, learning to hear and recognize the One True Voice when He spoke. Wonder and awe are at the forefront as we watch Him move in us, through us, and around us; where we move from glory to glory. And when we look back, we realize the glory all along was finding more of Him, for the process is not to just get us to our destination, it is a way of life. He is life, and He is our destination.

Looking through a decade of journals I've kept, I see the same theme over and over again. I now laugh, "Wow, the Lord is so patient with me. He has been drawing me closer to His heart as a daughter ever since I can remember."

I have been so wrapped up in self-protection, pushing—rushing—through the process, I wasn't able to see it. Every time I broke through a wall, I was met with another, and then another. At times, it felt like the wall was coming down, brick by brick. Other times, gone in an instant and forever. I can choose to be disappointed, learning the same things over again, or I can be grateful that I am deeper into the truth of His heart. This is our life, growing and falling deeper in love with Him until that day we meet face-to-face.

When we can finally embrace the process for what it truly is, we move forward in a brand-new way of life. Life becomes more enjoyable when we realize there is always something to learn that moves us closer to God's heart, exposing who we truly are and who we truly want to be.

I chose to embrace the process and said yes to God. I was tired of the struggle. Tired of talking about God and not experiencing Him and falling back into the same struggles and sins. I knew something had to change, and God placed it in my heart to accept His invitation to embrace the process.

I said, "Yes, okay. I see what you want, Lord, but now what?"

The Wrestle

"The degree to which a person can grow is in direct proportion to the amount of truth they can accept about themselves without running away." —Leland Val Van De Wall

I remember this hard conversation I had with a few friends. Thoughts and feelings surfaced that had been hidden over the years. In an honest moment, I learned that they didn't feel much compassion from me during a certain time of their lives. As they spoke, their words triggered me, and I shut down. All I could do was think about how to defend myself from what felt like accusations. This struggle began inside of me—fear fighting against my anger. Fear of being exposed and admitting my shortcomings and anger in my defense. I knew there were two choices when it was my turn to speak. What I wasn't expecting was the revelation and rush of emotions that would follow.

I responded, "You're right; I haven't given you grace"— (here came the revelation)—"because *I* wasn't given any grace and truly did not have the capacity for it for myself at the time." After expressing this, I wanted to hide my face in a pillow.

Having my first child was a very traumatic event. Forty-eight hours of labor that threatened to end in a C-section. I stayed in the hospital longer than usual because they wanted to monitor my heart. By the time I was sent home, my husband's paternity leave was up, and he had to go back to work. I had zero time to adjust to this new life or heal physically, and no real help around me. After six weeks of my own maternity leave, I jumped back into youth group, prayer room, worship, and leadership and conferences on Sundays. My baby was only four months old when I allowed myself to be guilted into being a chaperone for a youth group water park event. I felt trapped, unseen without a voice. I wasn't allowed to rest or just be—no, I had to get back to it, and that was exhausting. All of these thoughts and emotions flooded back to my memory as I admitted to my friends they were right. I couldn't extend any grace for them at the time, how could I? I didn't know how—even for myself. I was able to admit I wasn't as perfect as I tried to make myself out to be. This was a marking moment for me.

This is why the idea of being exposed for who I really was terrified me. To be seen as someone who is strong, disciplined, persistent, and fun, that's easy; but to allow people to see that I bleed easily, I'm sensitive, I care deeply, and I have battle scars that aren't fully healed caused me to lash out or shut down, even with those I loved.

Admitting I was jealous of those around me felt ugly and unacceptable. I knew something was off, and I would push these things down. Thoughts like, *What is wrong with me? Why can't I overcome this? Why can't I get a grip on this?* just wore me down.

The idea of being so insecure killed me! My heart was so tender toward the things of the Lord, and I wanted to be a part of others' healing journeys. But how could I help others heal when I was still functioning out of my own pain (and there had been so much) from my past that I didn't realize? At this time, it was my pride that shielded me and kept me safe, but the Lord wanted to be the one to keep me safe, to make me secure in Him. Although unsteady in each step, **I took the first one by embracing the process—admitting to my shortcomings.**

This didn't happen overnight, and that's okay. It's a journey. With that said, His standard is not our standard, His ways are much higher, and He will do "everything in abundance, more than you expect—life in its fullness until you overflow!" (John 10:10)

It is His glory that is revealed through our surrendered life. We must give Him our hearts and dare to believe that His goodness is always directed toward us—never ending.

Let His love draw you in, and show yourself fully to the Lord. This is how it was always meant to be.

I want to encourage you with this. Life will punch you in the gut, and more than once, at that. We all have childhood wounds that need to be processed. We all have toxic traits. We are not perfect and never will be. What I've learned through all this is the sooner I can admit that I don't know it all, that I'm not perfect, and that I have blemishes too, the easier it is to accept and love myself for being human. God never made us to hide our flaws from Him. We are born naked for a reason. There is something that happens within when we start to hide things. It opens the door for lies and isolation to creep in. It destroys relationships, and we become versions of ourselves we never intended to be. Know this: God already sees your weeds. He already sees the struggles of it all. You aren't actually hiding anything from Him. And the sooner we lay down our pride and self-protections (that we are aware of), the sooner healing can come in and we can come out from under them.

Jesus died because He loves you, and He loves you the same yesterday as He does today. Nothing you do today to make yourself better tomorrow will make God love you more. And when you do mess up or fear comes in and your hurt self comes out, He still loves you and is with you, waiting for you to come to Him. Do not hide from the One who gave you life. I know you are tired, but there is rest in Him. You don't have to pretend with Him—let it all out, and watch how His love comes rushing in.

As said by Todd White, founder and president of Lifestyle Christianity, "He doesn't just want our hearts; he wants our lives."

It starts with the understanding that the process is meant to develop you. It is to risk losing all the world has to offer you to gain all of Him.

Process Over Promise

What is a promise?

Promise

1. a declaration or assurance that one will do a particular thing or that a particular thing will happen.[3]

I had no idea what a promise from God was. I didn't know it was as simple as Him saying He'd do something. This caused confusion for me because I didn't know what God had actually promised me. I just knew I had desires in me that no matter how many times I tried to walk away from them, God always brought me back through constant opportunities to take them. What do you do when God has promised you something, but with every promise comes a process?

In the book of Genesis, a man named Jacob was brought through a long and grueling process to obtain his promise. Jacob was sent by his father to find a woman to marry among his uncle's daughters. Jacob fell in love with his uncle Laban's younger daughter, Rachel. The Bible describes Rachel and her older sister by saying, "There was no sparkle in Leah's eyes, but Rachel had a beautiful figure and a lovely face." Jacob then agreed to work for seven years if he could take Rachel as his wife. Jacob's love for Rachel was so intense that the seven years

---

[3] *Oxford Languages Google Online*

seemed but a couple of days. But on the night of the wedding, Jacob was tricked and given Leah as a wife instead. When he woke up, he saw Leah beside him. Upset, Jacob went to his uncle and asked, "Why have you tricked me?" Laban replied, "It's not our custom here to marry off a younger daughter ahead of the firstborn. But wait until the bridal week is over; then we'll give you Rachel, too—provided you promise to work another seven years for me." So, Jacob agreed to work seven more years. A week after Jacob had married Leah, Laban gave him Rachel, too" (Genesis 29:26-28 NLT).

Can you imagine? All those years of hard work, only to be given something you never wanted instead of what you truly worked hard for? And here, a sudden turn of events: "When the Lord saw that Leah was <u>unloved</u>, he enabled her to have children, but Rachel could not" (Genesis 29:31).

Why was Rachel's womb closed? Why was it so important that Leah was also loved? Could it be that God valued the process more than the promise? What is the point of the process? Is it merely to learn tools and skills that help us keep the promise once it is given? Or is it much more than that? Is the process for the promise or is it for your relationship with the Lord to grow and flourish?

When you go through the process, you will be confronted with what is truly going on in your heart.

Scripture says Leah had no sparkle in her eyes but immediately went on to say that Rachel had a beautiful figure. The process will very quickly expose your motives and who you are, even if you are not aware of it. What are you in this for? If you lost it all tomorrow, how would you respond? Are you going after it because it's pretty and it will make you feel and look good? Because I'm telling you, you will be tested, for God will always give you a Leah! How you respond when you don't get your way is a great indicator of motives.

Let's take worship leading as an example. Many view leading worship on the stage as "making it." But what do you do when you are off the stage? Do you only worship when it's your turn to lead on a Sunday, or do you worship God throughout the week as well? Now, I understand worship is more than music, but I want to hone in on a point. Is leading worship about the heart of worship, or is it about how it makes you feel and what you think about yourself? Maybe it's really how people perceive you and treat you once you are up on that stage. It could be to fill a void that's missing inside. My point is, what's the heart motive behind why you want to do what you want to do? Is it merely because it looks good, like Rachel? Or is there more depth to it?

Three times I went from background vocalist to leading worship, back to background vocalist again. I genuinely loved being a background singer. I loved the harmonies and supporting the leader. However, I grew up with a mic in my hand and a camera in my face. My dad carried a cam recorder everywhere he went, so I was no stranger to the stage. I quickly learned performing a song was nothing like singing a song where you were encouraged to follow the Spirit's leading or to spontaneously belt out what you thought He was saying in the middle of that song. I only knew leading put your voice on display and praise came from performance.

When given the opportunity, I discovered the very thing I desired was the same thing that terrified me. I was not confident in hearing God's voice. Yet the more confident I grew, the more I desired to be the lead. By the third time this happened, I was leading worship semi-regularly, for the better part of a year. I had gone through some major wrestling of the heart, knowing I was qualified to lead but also knowing it wasn't about the position, but about the heart of worship. I routinely reminded myself of this and my reason for being there, which was to worship Jesus. This struggle continued with God from the first moment I sang backup to the ups and downs as lead worship leader. My heart was constantly being exposed.

That's when the insecurities and lies would rise up about myself.

Kingdom Work

I love how God points out that Leah had no sparkle in her eyes. How often do God's blessings seem like commonplace, mundane, "nothing special" things? We think everyday life as less important and place more value on what something looks like and how we are perceived. We often ignore the importance of the heart work and mind transformation God is doing in us as we walk through each season. I believe the Lord wants to shift our minds to enjoy the process of doing life with Him by changing what we see as Kingdom Work. We have gotten too caught up in what Kingdom Work *should* look like instead of embracing whatever God has you doing. God put gifting, callings, and assignments on every person's life that are meant to be used in all areas of life. Wherever God has placed you, *is* Kingdom Work.

And finally, the process will confront your trust in God's timing. If you read the Bible, you will find numerous people who had to wait years or even decades before their promise came to pass.

Jacob is an example of that.

And what about King David? David began as a shepherd boy who tended to his father's sheep before he was anointed king. Once he was anointed king, he went right back to tending sheep. Now, doors of opportunity opened for David, like killing

Goliath, serving King Saul, and eventually fighting in the kings' army. Everything looked like David was making his way to the Kingdom nicely. However, God's favor on David's life caused jealously in Saul's heart, which sparked the beginning of a long wilderness journey for David, running from the king for many years. Though David's first wilderness prepared him to kill Goliath, his second wilderness prepared him for kingship as he was given men to lead, train, and pour his life into; a foreshadowing, if you will, of what would happen to him when he stepped into his promise as king.

The closer we think we are to the fulfillment of the promise, the more likely we are to face setbacks—and wind up taking ten steps backward. It looks like the promise, but it is actually preparation *for* the promise. Like a test and training, all at the same time. It can feel like a carrot hung in front of our face, just for it to be ripped away before we take a bite. Maybe you've felt like Jacob felt when he was tricked. Yet the purpose isn't trickery (like in Jacob's case) but instead preparation, integrity, trust, relationship, character, and growth. It's preparation and protection for the promise. It reveals where our identity lies—in just making it to the promise versus our identity being in God.

In this way, the promise won't crush us but instead causes us to thrive in God's faithfulness. Everything God does is from a place of love.

The process reveals not only where our identity lies but if we will steward or manage the things gained in it.

When we do not steward well what God has given us (Leah), He shuts the womb of our promise (Rachel).

Without the process, we miss out on the beauty of the journey and what God does in and through us along the way. We cannot hold onto the promise more than we hang on to the Promise Giver.

Did you know Jesus himself came out of Leah's bloodline and not Rachel's? **Jesus is found in the process.** Jesus wants to make sure we can sustain what He has given us and that we walk with Him in it. He wants us to build *with* Him, not *for* Him. He wants our motives, our heart, and our actions to be rooted *in* Him— and that takes time. He wants us to cling to Him in all things, no matter what life throws at us. That takes a process of one foot in front of the other, consistently moving forward. It takes relationship, embracing and learning to love Him in the day-to-day. To steward well the things in life that have no sparkle in them and to know that promise is birthed in the mundane. Trust me, you don't want the promise without the process. You don't want to get there, only to find out your character can't handle it; that you are vulnerable to the attacks of your enemies and lose yourself to the fear of man because you valued the destination more than the One who is taking you there.

Remember, the promise is the signpost that says, LOOK WHAT GOD DID. It is like the cherry on top and the place we make a memorial to remind us of His goodness and faithfulness.

The process is where we meet God. Where we learn to follow the cloud by day and fire by night; where we learn to strengthen ourselves in the Lord alone and rely on Him to provide our daily needs.

Chapter 2

THE POWER OF OUR THOUGHTS

"I can't afford to have thoughts in my head about me, that God doesn't have in His." —Bill Johnson[4]

My husband and I started our own business shortly after the pandemic hit. We made farmhouse signs, barn door gates and doors, and blanket ladders. I remember being afraid to succeed. I had a friend who thought that was the strangest thing. A lot of people are afraid to fail, but I was afraid to succeed. I leaned into that to see what was behind the fear. As I looked, I discovered it was rooted in the fear of failure. I couldn't stand the idea of people purchasing our products and hating them. What if it broke? What if I missed a spot painting or the lettering on the sign wasn't perfect and there was a little blemish? What if it was not as good as someone else they bought from?

If you hadn't noticed yet, I have some people pleasing tendencies. I had to let my husband determine the price of our work because if it was up to me, I would have given it all

---

[4] *Author, speaker and senior pastor of Bethel Church in Redding, California.*

away for free. Not really, but I sure didn't see the value in my time and energy. I knew this, but that didn't stop it.

Content creator Mason Denver nails this in his hilarious "Conversation of a Counselor and a Millennial" routine. The counselor begins with the subject repeating after him but changing key concepts.

"Repeat after me…"

"Okay."

"If it's not perfect…"

"If it's not perfect…"

"On the first try…"

"On the first try…"

"It's a learning opportunity, and I get to try again."

"It's trash, I'm trash, and I am NEVER trying that again."

"NO, where did you get that?"

"Probably somewhere in my childhood…I don't know!"

If this conversation doesn't sum up my experience, I'm not sure what does. There is an identity crisis and it's come to a tipping point. Will we learn to value ourselves and take action that goes against mindsets we've grown up with, or will we continue with what we've learned and known?

We all have subtle but destructive thoughts. Not the ones that come out of our mouths in conversations or when we mess up, but the ones we are not aware of that pass by unnoticed.

You know, the thoughts after you look in the mirror and are walking away that say, "I'll never lose the weight, what's the point?" or "Why is this so hard?" How about those thoughts when you find out your friend got the role or position you were hoping to get? You act really excited, but all you can think about is how you deserved that position and how unqualified you think your friend is for it. Or maybe your thoughts are the opposite, and now you are attacking yourself, your worth, and your value, and now rejection is shouting, "See, you're not good enough." These thoughts run rampant in our mind, unchecked most days. To be honest, unless you practice self-awareness, they are like ninjas in our brains.

Recognizing the Lies

In 2016, my husband and I went to Love After Marriage[5], a weeklong marriage retreat. It was then that the Lord introduced the importance of recognizing lies and knowing His truth. He began to reveal to me the power of our thoughts in His word, and my mind was awakened in a whole new perspective. He highlighted the power of mindsets to me in a story from the book of Matthew, when Jesus rebuked Peter. In chapter 16, Peter receives revelation of who Jesus is by saying, "You are the Anointed One, the Son of the living God." Because of this revelation, Jesus opens up about what was about to happen to Himself, how He would be killed and three days later be raised to life again. Shocked, Peter took Jesus aside to correct Him privately. He reprimanded Jesus over and over, saying to Him, "God forbid, Master! Spare yourself. You must never let this happen to you!" Jesus turned to Peter and said, "Get out of my way, you Satan! You are an offense to me, because your **thoughts** are only filled with man's viewpoint and not with *the ways of God.*" The New Living Translation says, "You are a dangerous trap to me," and the Amplified Bible says, "You are a stumbling block to me."

A couple things stood out in these passages. First, God is not saying Satan is *inside* Peter, but that the way he is thinking is *like* Satan. Why? Because Peter did not see the bigger picture.

---

[5] *Oxford Languages Google Online*

For Jesus to not go to the cross would mean there would be no redemption and reconciliation between man and God. Peter was not understanding God's ways and was getting in the way of love. I also wonder what Jesus was thinking when Peter said, "God forbid," when it was God's plan. Talk about a slap in the face. A truth is revealed here: our thoughts either bring us toward love or away from it. There is no in-between, and Jesus came to destroy anything that keeps His children from His love. How many of us have gotten frustrated because we thought our way was better than God's? Or because we decided to do it our own way when we didn't understand and trust Him?

In all this, we are turning from the ways of God and leaning into ourselves instead. Anything that leans away from God is leaning toward Satan. The second thing that stood out to me was how Peter's thoughts affected Jesus. Peter's way of thinking was an offense, dangerous, and a stumbling block to his relationship with Jesus. Our relationships are affected by our thoughts. When our thoughts are only on man's viewpoint and not God's, they become an offense, dangerous, or a stumbling block in our relationship with Him. Do you know how hard it is to receive from God when your belief is the opposite of what He wants to do in your life? I wonder what Peter was afraid of when he heard Jesus had to die? Was he afraid of being alone? Maybe he didn't think He could do what Jesus was calling him to without Him? Maybe he had abandonment trauma. I mean, he did deny Jesus three times. Here's the thing, when we don't renew our mind, we respond and act in the very way we are trying to break free from. Fear makes us do crazy things. **Our ugliest selves comes out when fear grips us, and lies are usually rooted in fear.**

It also shows that who we surround ourselves with matters. People speak into our lives. Their words have the power of death or life. One thing I have learned is who you run with in life DOES matter. Our hearts get connected to people, and their opinions matter to us.

Look at Jesus. He knew who He was and what He came to do—to die on the cross. He knew why the Father had sent Him. However, Peter failed, not truly understanding the plan or purpose, even though He walked with Jesus every day! Our friends may not see what we see or hear what God has said to us, personally. Their opinions may hinder our movement with the Lord. This is why standing on what God has said to us is important. Humans are really good at rationalizing our way out of things. We can find ourselves stagnant and comfortable very quickly, all in the name of loyalty and connection. There is nothing comfortable about death, and there is nothing comfortable about following Jesus. Discernment is key.

Jesus hand-picked his disciples, yet Judas followed his own agenda in betrayal. Peter, James, and John fell asleep, not grasping the urgency of the moment. And Peter, resisting God's will, rebuked His Lord. Jesus knows who, what, and why things hold us back. He also knows when people keep us from moving forward and growing. It doesn't mean people are bad, but for whatever reason, it's not serving His purpose at the time, and change is needed.

Stop and Ask

From time to time, we need to reflect and ask ourselves some questions when it comes to where we are and where we want to go.

Am I surrounding myself with people (or things) that will help me get where I want to go?

Am I growing toward love, or are fear, doubt, and frustration being echoed back to me?

What is the topic of my conversation…what God is doing or the latest gossip and the sins of others?

God tells us who we are, but Satan will always question it. Satan is the accuser of the believer. Be careful who and what you listen to. Don't allow your relationships to pull you away and make you stagnant, but choose relationships that pull you closer to Jesus. To live this life after Christ to continually die to our old mindsets and be transformed by the Holy Spirit. There is a standard and a way, but it is in His leading that we discover it.

Romans 12:2 (NLT) says, "Let God transform you into a new person by changing the way you think." The Passion Translation says it this way: "Be inwardly transformed by the Holy Spirit through a total reformation of how you think."

How we live life and respond to it is directly related to what we think—about ourselves, other people, and God. It shapes how we love and the motives behind our actions. Proverbs 4:23 says, "So above all, guard the affections of your heart, for they affect all that you are. Pay attention to the welfare of your innermost being, for from there flows the wellspring of life."

I wish I would have grasped this so much earlier in my life. That this is all a part of the wrestling. I let my mind conform to those old thoughts and feelings. I sought validation from others, but that wasn't what I needed. I needed to accept and love myself for who I was. Who God said I was. I carried things I was never supposed to carry, and that led me to try to control life around me, which included others as well. And when my inability to convince others to do the "right" thing didn't work, I let that reflect on who I thought I was as a person. My mind needed to be transformed. I needed to pay attention to what was happening in me to care for myself in a different way, a way led by the Holy Spirit and His word.

Adjust

How do we pay attention to the welfare of our innermost being? Let's start by asking ourselves, "How am I doing? How am I mentally? Spiritually? Physically?"

What would you say if a friend asked you these same questions? Is your answer, "I don't know?" What about when someone asks you how you are doing, do you often respond with, "I'm good"?

Knowing the answers to these questions, or at least taking time to discover them, is vital to understanding yourself. If we don't understand why we respond the way we do or what caused a reaction, then it makes it harder to change. Not just for the sake of change, but truly understanding and extending compassion to ourselves. Our emotional responses are signs along the road, trying to tell us something. If you woke up joyful, then ended the day irritated and grumpy, there was a bump along the road that still needs processing. What about when someone says something to you, and suddenly, there is a pit in your stomach, and you instantly detach from the conversation and get defensive? I bet it had less to do with what was actually said and more about what you thought about yourself or the situation in which you heard it. It probably points to pain in your past. Emotions are neither right or wrong, but indicators, revealing what our thoughts are truly saying.

"Do I really believe this or have I been conditioned to think this?"

"Do I really want to do this or am I doing it to be perceived as a good Christian (person)?"

"Is this something I want to do or am I doing it so as not to disappoint or upset someone?"

Honest questions help us get to know ourselves.

Fixed
1.   fastened securely in position.
2. predetermined and not subject to or able to be changed.

I've recently learned a little bit about the difference between a fixed mindset and a growth mindset. In short, thoughts such as, "This is how it is" or "There is nothing I can do about it; this is just the lot in life I've been given; I just need to accept it" correspond with a fixed mindset. It is a hopeless and powerless way to think and live. It gives power to our circumstances. This way of thinking is rooted in lies we believe, leaving no hope for future change, and is a slippery slope to a victim mentality. However, a growth mindset is one that continually moves forward. It is teachable, always wanting to grow and learn more. It says, "I'm not good at this *yet...*" It knows the power of hard work and roots out stinking thinking. It says, "Practice make progress, not perfection."

Proverbs 4:21 says, "Fill your thoughts with my words until they penetrate deep into your spirit." Fill your thoughts? What does that look like? Philippians 4:8 says, "So keep your thoughts continually fixed on all that is authentic and real, honorable and admirable, beautiful and respectful, pure and holy, merciful and kind. And fasten your thoughts on every glorious work of God, praising him always."

I've been teaching my kids about guarding their hearts by fixing their thoughts on good things. I ask them, "How do you guard your heart?" They respond with, "By protecting our eyes and ears." What we watch, listen to, and focus on all affect how we think. Our thoughts turn into actions, which then turn into habits, which form our character, and we reap from life that with which we have surrounded ourselves.

And it starts with one of two things. We either trade a truth for a lie or a lie for truth. There is always an exchange for one or the other. This starts in childhood. We partner with lies spoken over us. "You'll never amount to anything," or "You must be shy," or "You can't do that." The list goes on. We never knew anything was wrong with us until people pointed it out, giving us their opinions. Those thought patterns become a lens through which we view our world.

1, 2, 3, SKIDOO

During our time at LAM in Redding, California, my husband

and I were introduced to a technique called, "1,2,3, Scudo," switching our lies for God's truths. We had a beautiful time with the Lord, bringing to Him whatever we were struggling with. I brought my fear of being "too much" to the Lord. I often felt the fear that I was being *too* loud, *too* expressive, or even *too* honest with people. These lies pushed me to be so hyper aware of how people viewed me, which forced me to mold myself into a distorted version of who I was in hopes of being accepted by others. When I asked God what His truth was over my fear, He said, "I've made you to be kind and carefree, but strong and fierce." There is nothing like hearing the truth straight from the Father. Once I heard it, my job was to embrace His truth as my reality.

This lie of being "too much" is a perfect example of believing someone else's projection on my life. Was I too much? Did I make people feel uncomfortable? Maybe they didn't know how to handle someone who was free to be themselves, so they shut me down to make themselves feel more comfortable. Maybe I wasn't too honest. Maybe people didn't know how to handle the truth, or maybe it was the way I said things that hurt them. I got comments like, "Anna's brutally honest; too aggressive," or "She is just too intimidating."

People may have hurts and wounds and when triggered, instead of asking why they feel this way, they project this onto the other person. They are not reacting to what that person is actually saying, but rather acting upon their perception of it.

They may not even be aware of what's going on inside of them. They see the other person as "the problem."

So now, when I think that I am not enough, I bring it to the Lord and am honest with what is going on inside. Then, I repent for partnering with this lie, bring it to the cross, and break partnership with it. After I give the Lord the lie, I ask him to replace that lie with His truth over me. You see, in the Kingdom, there is always something to receive. The Lord never leaves us without, and He always gives us something for what the enemy stole. All we have to do is to bring any and all lies to Him, then receive His truth and embrace it as our new reality.

Behold[6]
To see or observe (a thing or person, especially a remarkable or impressive one); to perceive through sight.

Have you ever been asked, "Who are you becoming?" or "Are you the person Jesus called you to be?" Implying that you are the sole source of achieving Christ-likeness. I find that shame likes to show up when I hear this. I used to say, "Jesus is my becoming," because you become what you behold. Though true, the key word is "behold." Yet, we seem to miss that word and replace it with "doing."

---

[6] *https://www.merriam-webster.com/dictionary/behold*

I remember listening to someone talk about this idea of becoming and couldn't pinpoint why this didn't sit right. It was at that moment I was reminded of Abraham and Sarah. Did you know Abraham was called the Father of Many Nations before it was seen in his life? Which would imply he was already who God said he was before it was seen in his life. Now, there was obedience that had to take place, but what stood out to me was this: all he had to do was have faith and be intimate with his wife. The requirement is the same for you and me. To believe and be intimate with the Lord. When intimacy starts to feel like it's not enough, we try to rush things, striving for something God has already said was done (giving birth to an Ishmael instead of an Isaac). The waiting in between is designed to reveal our inabilities, faithlessness, and what we believe about ourselves and the Lord, leading us to ultimately rely solely on Him. We were never meant to carry the weight of the cross. And when we think thoughts like, "Why aren't I more like Christ? I guess it's because I keep messing up," we begin to bear the weight of the cross when that was already bore for us. It is by His grace that we are empowered to receive His truth, and it's by His grace that we keep it and walk in it.

When this pesky lie comes knocking again, I just give it back to the Father. There is no shame or guilt in having to do it once, twice, or a hundred times. We are all in a process of finding freedom in our lives. So, when lies knock at your door, keep telling them to bow to Jesus, and shut that door.

When you decide to follow the spirit, He will lead you to truth. He will lead you into a new way of thinking. He will pluck out anything that keeps you from love. He will never shame you for struggling with any lie. He will only keep telling you the truth and how He sees you in His eyes. Don't forget that. And know that as truth overtakes those lies, as your mind is renewed, you will start living differently. Your perceptions will change, and you will make choices from truth, fueling confidence, killing insecurities, and protecting you from the fear of what others think.

Chapter 3

DOES HE KNOW YOU?

"One thing that is more important than knowing God, is Him knowing you." —Bill Johnson

When I was five years old, I asked Jesus into my heart. I so wanted to make sure it "worked," that I did it every night for a week. It wasn't until I told my dad what I was doing that I learned I only had to do it once. After that, I do not remember ever being told anything more about Jesus. I grew up going to church and knowing church, but not Jesus. So much so, that my conversations with the Lord sounded more like complaining and me telling Him what I was going to do, and if He didn't like it then He'd better stop me. I was missing His side of the relationship. I did not know there was another side until I was in my 20s. I did not know that He wanted to walk and talk with me in my everyday life. You may be asking, "Didn't you read your Bible?" No, no, I didn't. Friend, I could not understand the Bible. My father would read to me from the King James Version when I was a kid, and my brain hurt from all the thees and thous. I told my dad once, "I didn't understand a word you just read." The Bible was something I never understood the importance of.

I think about all those years I believed in God but never really tapped into the relationship part of it. The verse that stands out to me is Luke 13:25-27: "Depart from me for I never knew you. Then they will reply, 'But Lord, we did this with you and walked with you as you taught us.' And he will reply...go away from me!"

This verse confused me. How can you do things for the Lord but He never knew you? This verse can cause fear, for He is talking to people who *think* they are in relationship with Him and find out they actually don't have one. I think the important part to focus on here is where it says, "…depart from me for **I never knew you.**"

Yet, the Bible says, "I knew you before I formed you in your mother's womb" (Jeremiah 1:5).

The Hebrew word here is, "Yada." It means, "to know by experience." Yada is so much more! Yada is an all-encompassing intimacy. Think of marriage. It's knowing, yes, but it's living life with someone, it's experiencing them, it's connecting with them on a vulnerable level, knowing their likes and dislikes, and daily communing with them. This kind of connection is cultivated, it's intentional, and it's daily.

Have we been taught to know (yada) God? Or have we been taught to know *about* Him?

"Because knowing the word of God and knowing God of the word are two different things." —Lou Engle[7]

"...Depart from me for I do not (<u>yada</u>) you."

It's as if God is saying, "I know you; I knew you before you were even born. But you did not let Me in. You are not vulnerable with Me; you don't talk to Me. You have read about Me and have head knowledge about Me like a teacher lecturing in a classroom, but you won't let Me in to see your heart. You won't spend time with Me just so I can be with you. I do not know you intimately, it's only superficial."

I realized at that moment I had been striving and working to prove myself to the Lord this whole time. Though I was sincere in my relationship with God, I hadn't realized how much was out of fear of not being enough for God. I was saddened and repented for working to earn His love, rather than allowing His love into the deepest parts of my life. And it's hard to admit that you've become the very thing you've been trying not to become. I didn't want to be a worker bee, I wanted to be a daughter. I realized I didn't know how to truly rest and receive God's love. It's crazy, because I'm the most afraid of what actually sets me free—if I'm willing to face it. I have struggled so much with thinking I'm not doing enough, which put me in a constant state of fear; then doing too much because of the fear of

---

[7] Lou Engle Ministries

missing what God had for me. It's like I'm on a scavenger hunt, frantically trying to find the clues and put the pieces together so I can find the next clue. Constantly living in lack of what I think I don't have and hoping that, if I can just figure out all the clues, maybe it will be enough to make me feel worthy to be called God's daughter. The treasure hunt is real, but God has already given us the map and everything we need to find the treasure— for the treasure was always Him. It's why Jesus died. Not so we could strive more to be with Him but so we could rest in Him knowing (*yada*) it is as simple as opening ourselves up to Him and inviting Him to walk this journey with us.

This is why I'm so passionate about encouraging people to let God in. I think religion has done us an injustice when it comes to walking out this relationship with God. We haven't been taught to let Him know us. To let him in. To voice our pain, frustration, questions, and disappointments of life with Him, along with our joys, happiness, and victories. It really is that simple.

A Courageous Risk

So, how do we let God know us? I love how author Ray Leight says it: "*You will only get out of a relationship which you are willing to be vulnerable.*" To be vulnerable is to allow someone to see into your heart, expressing the core of your thoughts and emotions. We often think of vulnerability as a sign of defenselessness, yet being vulnerable is also a sign of courage and trust. Trust that God will protect those tender areas we share with Him. That He will transform us.

"For when I am weak [in human strength], then I am strong [truly able, truly powerful, truly drawing from God's strength]" (2 Cor. 12:10 AMP).

Whether in your frustrations or celebrations, let Him see into your heart. Your heart, the most precious thing you have. It's where love, emotions, and pain are held. Are you willing to give it to Him? To allow him to search it and shine light on anything that is holding you back from His love?

It has always been about a transparent, authentic relationship and a heart-to-heart connection between you and the Father. What if you said yes to the One who said yes to you? What if you gave Him your heart and let Him see into you? What if you dared to believe His goodness for you was never-ending? Letting His love draw you, not hiding anything, how it was always meant to be. Will you trust Him with your heart? Will you believe He is the safest, most trustworthy person to hold the most precious thing you have to give?

Take His hand. Look into the eyes of love and say, "Yes!" You won't regret it. He is drawing you, do you feel it? Can you hear Him calling, "Come be with me?"

I Said Yes, Now What?

Here are five practical ways that I've learned to let the Lord in to know me.

1. **Make time for Him every day.** Whenever works best for you. Don't allow people to guilt you into a certain time of day, to prove you are putting God first. Let the Lord lead you. Start with 15 minutes. If it goes longer, great. If life happens, move on, you have tomorrow.

2. **Start a journal.** I love to journal. I write as if I'm speaking right to the Lord. I express everything in it. I color-code entries. Black for my writing, green for verses that stand out to me, blue for dreams I've had, purple for dream interpretations, orange for prophetic words I feel God is speaking over me, and pink for random things. This makes it easier for me to find things in my journals. This habit teaches me to share every detail of my life, to steward what He is speaking to me, and keeps me organized.

3. **Turn your affections toward Him.** Just like with journaling, I do this throughout my day. Instead of having conversations in my head with myself, I direct it toward Him and talk to Him. I'll randomly tell Him I love Him. I'll even invite Him to go on walks with me! I'll ask Him His thoughts and whatever comes to mind. It's not complicated, it's just being aware of Him.

4. **Get into the habit of running to Him first, before people.**
As women, we like to process out loud and have someone
validate our feelings. There's nothing wrong with that, but if
we are not careful, what started out as sharing our pain can
turn into gossip, putting others down. When we practice
bringing things to the Lord first, we are letting Him know we
trust Him, giving Him first chance to speak into us about the
situation. Don't hold back but be honest with your thoughts
and big emotions. Trust that God can handle them.

5. **Worship.** This is a double-edged sword. Though worship is
about God and loving on Him for who He is, it is also a great time
to communicate through expression. Sing, play, dance, draw,
soak—you pick. Not only does this clear our head, but it brings
us back to zero. We step into our true selves when everything
is fixed on Him. It's a double-edged sword because He is always
singing back to us because of His great love. He cannot help but
respond to His children. I have had many encounters where the
Lord just washed over me as I worshiped Him. I cry as what I
was singing hit my spirit. I'll physically feel His presence over
my entire being. I walk away changed, all because I came to
worship and process my emotions with Him.

Transformation

This has changed my life, and I hear God more clearly now. I
see him in everything. I've learned that what I sow in my quiet

times speaks to me throughout the day or week. Once, I asked God a question in my quiet time, and later that same day, I was watching a sermon, and it was all about my question. Don't brush coincidence off. I have found it's God speaking into our daily lives.

It has been in letting God in, knowing Him, and Him knowing me in a Yada way, that He now has access to reveal Himself to me. Relationships take time to build. God is so patient as to give us that time to build a relationship with Him. As we let Him in, He lets us in, and the more we see of Him, the more we want to give ourselves to Him.

This love has changed me as a person in more ways than I can say.

I used to be such an angry mother. I never knew I had anger until I had two kids. The constant needing, the constant boundary crossing, and the constant not listening was more than I could take. I found myself screaming and throwing things at the wall when I felt powerless to get my kids to go to bed. I didn't realize I was in so much pain from years of not being heard or feeling seen. I was so focused on the behavior that I was missing the healing. I was trying to be a good daughter and better parent, all to be accepted by God. It wasn't until I admitted that I had an anger issue that God came in and helped me walk through it. God showed me where in my childhood boundaries were crossed and where people screamed at me and embarrassed me. Through a seven-year journey, God revealed to me lies and past events that were the root of my outward self defenses. Most pivotal, though, was learning that I didn't have to prove anything. I just had to bring to Him my heart and show Him what was hurting. He is so good to heal those hurts because He loves us so fiercely. Love transforms you in the best of ways.

Now when my kids cross my boundaries or I get upset, I've learned to give myself grace, knowing there is still more healing to come. If there's one thing kids know how to do, it's show you where pain still resides and humble you, bringing with it many apologies.

When we are loved, love is what comes flowing out. Control then loses its grip, fear is drowned out, and rejection's sting is replaced with acceptance by the one who made us.

All because we took the risk of letting love in.

Chapter 4

FOLLOW HIS LEADING

"If you want to be like Him, invest in yourself and see your value." —Ray Leight

Do you value yourself the same way you value others?

Have you ever had a conversation with a friend who was hurt by someone who disregarded their boundaries? You then encouraged your friend to go to that person, letting them know how they feel. Or you told them not to allow others to "walk all over them"?

But…when it comes to YOU and people who disregard your boundaries, that same advice goes out the window. When it comes to *you*, you allow people to step all over you. You don't go talk to them and tell them how you feel because you think it doesn't matter.

Where did all that passion and zeal you had for your friend go when it came to *you*?

When I was pregnant with my second son, I took a risk and found a new local hair salon. My stylist, who I had gone to for over a decade, lived over an hour and a half away from me. I didn't want to go that far unless it was a big event. So, I took a chance on this place. I ended up getting an inexperienced stylist and was too afraid to spend the money on what I really wanted, so things got off to a bad start.

To make things worse, I struggled to explain how I wanted my hair to be cut—you know, how MY hair stylist does it. This left the new stylist confused.

I left frustrated and dissatisfied. Afterward, I just sat in my car and cried.

And you know what? I was going to leave it like that. I was going to choose to have this haircut I did not like and live with it while complaining about it. I'm so thankful for my husband and sister-in-law, who encouraged me to call them back and have them fix it.

I stuck up for myself. I did something that day that was hard, but I chose to value myself and through my actions said, "I matter."

How many of us neglect what we put into our bodies, but the minute we get pregnant, we insist on organic and check each label on everything we eat? After the baby is born, we go back to eating whatever we want. Do we really see the baby as more valuable than ourselves? Do we use the baby as an excuse to value ourselves because we can't do it without a reason outside of ourselves?

As women, we have been so conditioned to take care of everyone else around us but ourselves. We wear the hats of wife, mom, friend, housekeeper, Uber driver, event planner. And what if you are a working mom on top of all that? We are asked to pour out, and rarely does anyone fight to fill us back up. We often believe our value comes from whether everyone in our life is happy and well taken care of.

We have been brainwashed to think that what a woman does at home is less valuable because it doesn't reap the reward of a *paycheck*.

All of this **is** work—at home. How can we show up for our spouse and our kids when we are not mentally and physically healthy? This is why the "self-love movement" is so loud. Women have had enough. They are trying to say, "What I need matters, too." Though I don't agree with all of this movement, I do believe it has sparked some valid questions we need to ask ourselves as women.

Do we value and champion ourselves like we do others? Do we value ourselves enough to have those hard conversations when our feelings are hurt? Do we ask for time off to go enjoy coffee with a friend? Do we think we are worth the money spent to take a weekend trip away or to get a massage?

I remember the days I had to fight to get a couple hours to myself outside of the house. The guilt that followed me because I was leaving my two kids home with my husband was awful. And the subtle, passive aggressive comments said when I would spend thirty dollars on a blouse. Or the shame that filled my mind when I heard, "Geez, you're an expensive woman."

My husband and I have come a long way from those days, but it started with investing in myself in small ways and having those hard conversations.

Do you think you're worth the money, the time, the "break"? If not, who told you you weren't? If you don't know the answer to that question, it might be time for some healing.

Step into Healing

There was a time in my healing journey I evaluated whether or not I thought my pain mattered.

I processed those thoughts with a poem:

Hurting pieces of me on the floor. I am staring at them; I don't know what to do. Do I tape or glue them? Should I rearrange them? Then I see your hand reaching out. I take hold, and you pull me close as we start to dance. Forgetting the hurting pieces I left back on shore. How could I remember when I'm lost in your eyes? Filled with wonder and awe as you lead me into the deep.

Suddenly, it goes quiet. The noise of the shore silenced. I can finally hear clearly. In the deep, our hearts sync. This is identity. This is knowing. This is the heartbeat of heaven. You and me, and me and you, dancing.

It is in the Father's heart for us to live life out of wholeness. He has already created us in His image, now we are in the process of believing His reality over us. We often look at the hurting places in our hearts and think we are broken and not valuable, but that just isn't the case. Our hearts are hurting from life happening to us, but there is healing, restoration, and freedom available from the pain surrounding us. God cares deeply about our wounds and the places we boarded up with lock and key. He wants to open the window and shed light on the lies we are believing; to show us it's not so scary. He wants to love us back to our true identity, to reveal to us that He sees us.

Open the windows, kick up the dust, blow it outside, and revive my heart again. That was my cry. I just wanted to stop hiding behind pain. I wanted His truth to shine on my hurt, even if all I could do was open a window in hopes to work my way to opening the door to my heart.

We cannot love Him without allowing Him to love on us. To show love, we must spend time with Love. When the Bible says to "love your friend in the same way you love yourself," you cannot do this without first loving yourself. And if you don't spend time **with** Love, the One who created you, formed you, and shaped you in your mother's womb, then how can you love yourself? How can we value ourselves when we don't see how much He values us? It is in receiving the love of the Father that we can believe His love for us.

"I love each of you with the same love that the Father loves me. You must continually let my love nourish your hearts" (John 15:9).

He is passionate about His relationship with you!

"We love because He first loved us" (1 John 4:19).

You Choose

Part of having a Christ-like mindset is seeing yourself like He sees you.

For me, it started when I read *Boundaries* by Dr. Henry Cloud. This book gave me permission to take care of myself. It showed me that I am only responsible for myself and not how others respond to me. At that time, my marriage was a wreck.

We were screaming at each other, slamming doors, using intimidation and anger. Once, I stormed out of the house to the park and just sat there, listening to worship music until I could calm down.

Oh, the anger! Our tender hearts hurting, not knowing how to express the pain. Covered in guilt and shame from being trapped in a lie, not knowing how to make it all stop. I wanted to love my husband and be loved by him. The problem was, I didn't know how to love myself. I would try and then quit because I didn't see any change in him. It was a "do-to-get" mindset instead of a "love-without-strings" one. I had nothing to give because there was nothing inside to give from. It wasn't until I began setting boundaries with my husband, no longer allowing him to use words to hurt me in arguments, that things started to change. When we invest in ourselves for healing, the world around us starts to change.

Our marriage was a huge uphill battle the first five years. I remember eating at Cracker Barrel with my grandma, crying because I thought I had married the wrong man. You see, my husband and I weren't head over heels in love with each other. It was more like a knowing—that he was for me, and I was for him. I always say, "We didn't fall in love, we fought for love." Every time we planned time away, a day or two before we'd leave, we would get into such an argument it would ruin our time together. I'd question myself. Is it me? Is something wrong with me that this keeps happening? This isn't normal.

How come my husband doesn't pursue me? I would even have dreams of him cheating on me. I'd brush them off—but deep down inside I wondered, is he being unfaithful?

The tools we learned at LAM were so valuable at this key time in our marriage. During this time, my husband's porn addiction came to light. Thank God we were up in Redding at the retreat when it did! We could unpack the pain and hurt, and for me, the rejection of all this, among loving, understanding people.

I tried everything to fix what I thought was an external problem, not realizing it was an internal one. My husband's struggle to be set free from the porn addiction brought him so much guilt. He had feelings of unworthiness and heaviness—shame, telling him, "You should know better because you're a pastor's kid; how could you?" Yet, he carried it alone, isolated, with no one to talk to; hidden in the dark, not knowing how to get out of this sin that had entrapped him. He felt so unworthy of loving me. I never knew he struggled with this the whole time. I was thankful it came out in a place that felt safe for us both to process all those big emotions and that we had the support to help us walk through it all.

Take the First Step

It was only when we dug deep into those hurting places in our hearts that healing and freedom broke through. We had to allow ourselves to be vulnerable and honest about the state of our hearts and step out of the shadow of isolation, shame, guilt, and into the light, letting it illuminate everything. Friend, those thoughts that haunt you and keep you from opening up to someone, thoughts that say, "They will leave if you tell them and will never look at you the same" or "This is too big or too bad, you can't let people see," are all lies from the enemy to keep you bound in shame and guilt. They make you think you are unworthy of love and affection and that you deserve to suffer because of what happened. Stop punishing yourself, forgive yourself for what you've done. The feelings are very real, but the thoughts that go with those emotions are lies. If this is you, and you don't think you have any safe people around you, I encourage you to seek help. Either through counseling, a Sozo[8] (a unique ministry where people partner with you and the Holy Spirit to reveal lies and bring healing), Identity Coaching[9] (which is similar to Sozo), or any other way you can express and process in a safe environment. Anything that will help you take the steps toward healing.

When Jesus died on that cross, He made you valuable. He defines your worth. He gave His life so that you may be covered in righteousness, grace, beauty, and holiness. He paid for your sins, past, present, and future. He paid it all on that cross. It is

_____

[8] *Sozo" is a Greek word which is translated in the Bible as "to heal," "to save," or "to make whole" (Mark 5:23 and 28). It also means complete freedom and wholeness in spirit, soul, and body.*
[9] *Challenges self beliefs and brings a new perspective, resulting in new life choices.*

only for you to believe that His blood was enough to restore all. When we say yes to Him, He makes us new—completely new! The past is washed away, never to be thought about again. Gone. Forever. The power of sin is broken. Picture Jesus's death on the cross, taking our sins and drowning them in His blood. He takes our sins and holds them under the blood— never to be remembered again. This is how He showers us in His grace, grace that empowers us through each and every day. He doesn't see us like we think He sees us. No, He looks at us with eyes of love, tender devotion, and kindness. There is nothing we can do or say that will earn His love, acceptance, salvation, grace, or gifts. All we have to do is believe He is who He says He is.

Here is the hard truth: no one can make you fall in love with Jesus. No one can force you to follow the leading of the Holy Spirit. No one can make you use the tools to help you in your healing. Only you have the power to make that choice and put action to it. God leads us to healing, He IS healing. He may lead you to His word or a song, a book or a message, podcast, or a friend. His ways are endless, and healing comes in all shapes and sizes—if we are willing to follow where He leads and put action to it.

"Faith without action is dead" (James 2:17). Or, as I like to say, "Trust without action is dead."

I have watched people struggle to choose to do the work when it comes to inner healing. The reasons are always different. "I don't want to go back into the past," or " I don't think it will work." Fear or pride hinders them. We have allowed the lies of our past or what people have put on us, to keep us stuck. We partner with them and choose to embrace them. We allow the pain of the past to keep us from moving forward. We say, "GOD, I'LL GIVE YOU MY LIFE! But not this part. Everything but that." My question to you is, "Do you trust God? Do you trust Him with your pain, your past, and your future? Or will you continue to allow self-protection to keep you safe?" Wherever there is self-protection, God cannot be. You have closed yourself off to the truth that would set you free.

The Passion Translation says in 2 Corinthians 3:17, "Wherever he is Lord, there is freedom."

Did you catch it?

Wherever YOU make Him Lord, there is freedom. He doesn't just want our hearts, He wants our lives. But to have our lives, we must allow Him to love every part it. There is only true freedom in those places where He is Lord and truth reigns. Allow Him to see into every corner.

EVERY part.

Every shadow.

Every locked door.

Everything to be touched by His love and light.

The first of the Ten Commandments says, "Love the Lord your God with every passion of your heart, with all the energy of your being, and with every thought that is within you" (Matt. 22:37).

If we were to love Him like He loved us, it would require that we give all of our heart and all of our lives. It's the great exchange. All of Him for all of me. When we say yes to Him, we are saying yes to a covenant relationship with Jesus, and He will not share his bride with any other.

"He knows we are His since He has stamped His seal of love over our hearts and has given us the Holy Spirit like an engagement ring is given to a bride—a down payment of the blessings to come!" (2 Cor. 1:22)

Oh, how He loves you!

So today, will you fall into love? Will you allow the Father that is Love to love on you today? Stop and wait on Him. You don't have to prove or do anything, but just be; be with Him and allow His love to wash over you. It takes but one moment to turn to the Lord with an open heart. When we do this, the veil is lifted, truth comes in, and suddenly, we see.

Prayer

"Lord, show me how to put my guard down. Show me how to open up my heart to receive this love you have for me. I'll open up my heart. Would you come and see, come and heal, all of me so I can love you wholeheartedly? I give you permission to see every detail of my heart. Show me the truth, all the lies I've been believing. May your awakening breath blow upon my life until I am fully yours. Blow your healing, your love, and your truth into me. Spare nothing; hold nothing back, until I am fully yours. I want to love you with ALL of me. Every scar, every bruise, and every part that hurts and is sensitive to the touch. I'll show you my heart, for I know you are a safe place to fall apart."

Chapter 5

LEARNING TO RECEIVE

"We love because He first loved us" (1 John 4:19).

What do you think of when you hear the word "receiving"?

Do you get excited? Does a memory come up? Are they happy thoughts that surround receiving? Or do panic and anxiety come first? Does it stress you out? I've always enjoyed the idea of receiving. I think about Christmas as a kid and the joy of opening presents. However, as an adult, thinking about how nice it would be to be given a gift and actually receiving a gift are two different experiences.

Once, I was having coffee with a friend, and she wanted to pay for me. I said, "No, I got it, don't worry about me." When someone wants to pay for you or give you something, and you respond by saying, "Oh, no, I got it; don't worry about me," you probably don't know how to receive well. So when my friend responded with, "Are you going to rob me of blessing you?" it hit me hard. Sheesh! Uh, well, when you say it like that…

Do you know how many blessings we have missed out on just because we were unable or unwilling to receive from others and God? Yikes! For me, it was a self-worth and performance issue. If I could not work for it, then I didn't deserve it. And if I did receive it, I would make sure to "even the score" next time. The more expensive the gift, the harder it was for me to receive. If I can't pay it back, then I can't receive it. Well, if we can work for it, then it's not truly a gift, and how many things in the Kingdom of Heaven are given freely?

Salvation is a gift, grace is a gift, mercy is a gift, love is a gift, and even the "gifts" are gifts. If we can't receive from others here on Earth, how then will we receive what Jesus has freely given us? Daughters and Sons don't perform or pay for love, yet this is how most of us live.

What about receiving compliments or being celebrated? Do you gladly receive them and say thank you? Or do you brush them off as if it was no big deal? Maybe you respond with false humility, "Oh, it wasn't me, it was all God."

When I was younger, I couldn't give a compliment let alone receive one. Still, I craved the validation of them. I found that even though I had a hard time receiving compliments from others, I couldn't get enough of them. I didn't know it then, but my self-worth was down the drain. I thought if I wanted to receive, I had to do something first. I learned to perform. That's why when we hear one negative criticism about ourselves amongst the hundreds of compliments, we suck on it like a pacifier. Could it be that we believe the criticism over the compliment because we are so critical of ourselves? It's easier to believe the criticism because it is playing in the background of our subconscious every day. It's one thing to take constructive criticism and use it for improvement, but it's another when we can't let it go—or worse, having to prove ourselves or perform in order to change someone's mind, in a desperate attempt to control peoples' perceptions of us.

Believe that you are worth being celebrated and that you are still worth loving even when you mess up. You are still worthy of love in every stage of your journey. You can learn to love yourself in the midst of others' thoughts and opinions of you.

Art of Listening

How do you feel when you hear the words, "God loves you"?

What goes through your mind when I tell you God says that you are "beauty itself" to Him?

Did you pay attention? Did you cringe? Did you tear up? Maybe you felt nothing. What if you heard those words directly from God? Do you think it would impact you differently than simply reading it or hearing it from someone else? In John 8:47, Jesus says, "If you really knew God, you would listen, *receive*, and respond with faith to his words." Most of us don't get past the listening part. We live in a world that doesn't know how to slow down enough for us to know ourselves, let alone to know our God. Jesus knew who He was. John 8:14 says, "For I absolutely know who I am, where I've come from, and where I am going."

If Jesus knew who He was, it's time for you to know who He says you are through His word.

So, I ask you, do you receive from God? Is it easy for you to receive? Or does it hurt to receive? When we aren't receiving, we are believing a lie, somewhere. Receiving for ourselves is not selfish. Let me be very clear: **to receive is not selfish, nor is loving yourself.** To love yourself is to bring glory to God. How? If we were made in the likeness of God and we reject that likeness, we will not shine the light that is Christ within. When we see ourselves the way Christ does, we are in awe of his beautiful design that is us and all humanity. We learn how amazing and majestic God is because He sees beauty in every single one of us. We all shine a different facet of God. If the four creatures in chapter four of the book of Revelation have been singing holy, holy, holy, all this time and haven't seen all there is to see in God, imagine how much there is to see, learn, and know about Him. Yet, God has chosen to reveal Himself through His children.

Have you ever been on an airplane and the flight attendant says to put on your oxygen mask first before assisting someone else? Why do we live life as if we are supposed to help the whole plane first before putting on our own oxygen mask? We live life as though it's not about us and wonder why we are drowning in anxiety and depression.

The Bible is filled with the word *overflow*. But to overflow would require that you have something to give. To truly help those around you, you cannot be empty, having given it all away, but you give from a place of overflow, from an overflow of love and peace. You can only do this once you have learned to receive, which means turning things inward for a little while. You can't give out of a place of pain, trauma, hurt, betrayal, or self-hatred. Those things need love and attention, or that is what you will give out. There is a saying, *"If you don't heal what hurt you, you will bleed on those who didn't cut you."* Receive love and healing for yourself so you can overflow from love with no strings attached. We are told to give away what we freely receive, but you need to know what you are giving away.

The Key

We cannot become brighter and brighter into the likeness of Christ when we are afraid or ashamed to embrace and love ourselves. It's not selfish, it's required. It's required if we are to love God with all our heart, all our body, all our mind, and all our spirit. I'm so tired of living small, all because I've been sold a lie that to live as Christ is to suffer in all areas of my life. Have you, too, been suffering in your mental health, in your physical health, in your spiritual health by submitting to things that appear righteous and holy but completely lack any value in making you more like Jesus? (Colossians 2:22)

I have always been a rule follower. I was afraid of making mistakes. Inner voices lied to me, telling me I didn't have what it takes. So, I stayed small and didn't make a sound; it's how I played along. People told me, "Don't rock the boat, you'll only end up drowning."

I didn't think I was worth the gift God had given to me. I didn't realize my pain, turned into pride, was protecting me. It's hard to overflow when we won't allow anything in. It's even harder to believe Jesus gave his life for you when you can't or won't receive a simple free cup of coffee from a friend. We fail to understand the cost Jesus made for us. Jesus died on that cross to purchase wholeness in every area of our lives, whether we receive it, believe it, or embrace it for ourselves.

Resilience is Learning to Face Pain

With that said, I believe it is time to understand ourselves. Luke 12:34 says, *"Where you deposit your treasure, that is where you fix your thoughts—and your heart will long to be there also."* I believe this beautiful verse allows us to take inventory of where our thoughts go and where we spend our time, energy, and money. Friend, we were made for more than just scrolling on social media to numb the pain of life or spending money on the next useless fad or object we think we need. There is nothing wrong with this, per sé, but we were made to live life more *abundantly*. We were made to drive, not simply be a passenger in life; *to take the bull by the horns*, so to speak.

Think about this for a moment. Wherever you deposit your treasure, that is where you fix your thoughts, and so your heart will long to be there. Is our treasure spent on avoiding our pain? Or is our treasure in facing and healing our pain? If our thoughts are constantly protecting us from our past, then we aren't free to dream. You know how many times I've had to apologize to my heart because I allowed fear to silence it out for years?

The goal is to get our mind and heart on the same page. That's hard when our mind is trapped in pain and self-protection. It doesn't mean you need to go looking for trouble, but it is an invitation to be aware of your thoughts and seek healing in places of pain you are already aware of. Consider this: when we choose to numb and ignore our pain, we are actually living a self-focused life. Our energy is spent in protecting ourselves, not realizing we are holding ourselves back.

For me, it hasn't been easy, but it has been truly worth it. The more I invest in myself and face my pain, the more alive I feel. I am on the road to self-acceptance. When we don't accept ourselves, it's a type of self-hatred. It's what keeps us from receiving love.

Do it Afraid

Have you ever done what scared you and then realized it wasn't as scary or as hard as you thought? And with practice and consistency, it becomes easier and easier to do.

One day, you look back wondering why it ever scared you in the first place. Facing your pain is no different. It's scary at first, and maybe you can only take it in small doses. But as you practice facing and processing it, you learn that it's not so scary and actually makes you stronger. You grow in ways you never thought possible.

Think about Jesus. How was he able to face such pain and suffering? He did not even defend himself but instead let it all happen. The Bible says in Hebrews 12:2, "For the joy set before Him, He endured the cross." WE were that joy. His great love for us compelled Him (John 3:16). "I love each of you with the same love that the Father loves me…for I continually live nourished and empowered by His love" (John 15:9-10).

He knew who He was. He knew how loved He was by the Father. He knew that He could face his pain because He knew who was walking through it with Him. Jesus was able to face

His pain, even unto death. That gives me hope. If Jesus can do it until death, then I know Jesus can help me face whatever comes my way. If I'm willing to face whatever hurt me, not only will I be able to endure, but it will bring me closer to the One who faced such great suffering, who will never leave me to walk through it alone. As you learn to face your pain, step by step, remember,

"If God is for you then who can be against you?" (Rom. 8:31)

Chapter 6

THE SECRET PLACE

"It is in the secret place where God begins to unfold His mysteries to your spirit. It is in the secret place where you get to discover who you are in Christ."—Smith Wigglesworth[10]

How do we learn to move forward with God once we have said yes? Welcome to the Secret Place. It's where we prioritize our relationship with the Lord and say, "You are worth making time for." When I think about the Secret Place with the Lord, I think of a place where it is just me and Him. I think of Song of Songs 4:16:

"Breathe on my garden with your spirit-wind. Stir up the sweet spice of your life within me. Spare nothing as you make me your fruitful garden. Hold nothing back until I release your fragrance. Come walk with me as you walked with Adam in your paradise garden. Come taste the fruits of your life in me."

I think about the way I feel and how I come undone when His truth and love overwhelm me. His weighty glory rests on me as

---

[10] *British evangelist who was influential in the early history of Pentecostalism.*

I worship Him. Worshipping with music is my favorite Secret Place time. The way my spirit responds, the excitement as I wait for His words to burst forth from me. His presence makes me weep, and all I feel is His love. In those moments, I know He is renewing my mind. The anticipation that He will show up in ways I don't have words for; feelings that can't be described.

How can I explain all the joys of the Secret Place, the joy in discovering His goodness and choosing intimacy with Him? Such a mystery, enjoying little glimpses as He leads us deeper into Him. I wish I could tell you step-by-step or give you a manual to follow, but it will be different for you as you experience the Secret Place for yourself.

The Secret Place isn't always magical. It may feel silly or like a waste of time when you have a preconceived idea of what it should look like. Many times, I have fallen asleep talking to God. Giving my best effort to be with Him, only to close my eyes and wake up to my children playing around me. Lies would rush in, saying, "You couldn't stay up because you don't think He is important enough. You failed Him, and He is so disappointed in you."

One day, I was listening to Bill Johnson, and he said, "I've never gotten mad at my children for falling asleep in my lap." My eyes filled with tears at this truth. How I needed to believe that because for too long, I had been condemning myself for not being good enough.

For me, the Secret Place is now where I come just to be close to Him. I can cry my feelings out, take refuge, and find a safe place when my whole world is tumbling down. He is there for me, even when I question everything. This has not been an instant fix. It has taken years of running to Him in everything to be able to look back and finally see He has never left me, never once betrayed, belittled, nor rejected me, nor chosen anyone else over me. He has always pulled me closer and loved me deeper.

My Secret Place has looked different throughout the years. It ebbs and flows with the seasons of my life. I used to think it had to be a certain chunk of time spent in solitude, otherwise if I didn't get that "time" with the Lord then it wasn't really time with Him. I couldn't feel peace because it HAD to look a certain way, like there was this formula. I've come to learn the Secret Place can be anywhere you've turned your affections toward Him. The Lord just wants to be with us. That's why it can happen anytime and anywhere.

Back in the day when I used to work at Jimmy John's, I used to open up the store. It was a four-hour process, but it was my favorite time of the day. I would blast worship music and just sing my little heart out while I cut veggies and baked bread. As I got older and had kids, I needed to be more creative in how I would spend time with the Lord. I've gone through seasons of waking up before the kids or going to a coffee shop down the road so I could get some "me and Jesus" time without the noise or distractions.

Other times, it's been playing my piano and worshipping during the kids' nap time. Now I just do it while they all play around me. They've gotten older now and need less of my attention, and I have become more flexible. I've also become more balanced with getting my needs met and getting the breaks I need so I'm not so desperate for the silence. Throughout the years, despite the challenges of how and when, most of the time it has looked like me and a cup of coffee, sitting with the Lord. Journaling is usually involved. Every once in a while, God will lead me to a book or a message during our time. I just try to be open and sensitive when I'm with Him. Sometimes, it's just silence, and I practice quieting my mind from all the distractions. There are even times it's spent following those bunny trails to inspired writing or dreams He has for me. It doesn't have to look like much, and it doesn't have to look like anyone else's, but it does have to look like something. Even if it's time spent on your commute or while you do the dishes.

The intimate and deep experiences of the Secret Place will be found by you as you choose to spend time with Him.

Vulnerability

1. the quality or state of being exposed (to the possibility of being attacked or harmed, either physically or emotionally)

"Vulnerability is uncertainty, risk, and emotional exposure." –Brene Brown

You know what I've found to be most effective in the Secret Place? Vulnerability. This has truly been key to every place in my journey. I don't know about you, but I always *saw* myself as being vulnerable. I was honest, told people the truth when they asked, and was very open about things going on in my life. I may be honest, and maybe even transparent, but I was not vulnerable. I am a very independent "self-sustained" person. My mindset was, I don't need people, therefore, I wouldn't share or expose what was happening inside the depths of me. When I did share myself, it never ended well.

My feelings weren't validated often as I was growing up. Singing and dancing since I was three years old, I was critiqued for everything I did. I was excited to perform, but it would inevitably be criticized.

When I didn't hear the love and encouragement I needed, I'd get angry and frustrated and walk away. I didn't understand myself enough to express how I felt. I hid my emotions, not letting anyone in.

When I was eight years old, I was told I was "too loud" for my friends. I handled it by hiding behind the couch, holding back my tears. Not until I composed myself did I come out, but then I acted like everything was okay. A little light went on in my mind: "You can't show people your pain." So, I never addressed my emotions and kept pushing them down until I eventually couldn't push them down anymore. The result was an emotional pendulum swing when I became an adult. People closest to me would hurt me, my anger would burst out, and I'd tell them what I really thought of them.

Every time I felt hurt, those pent up feelings would surface and erupt, building a case to why they were not a safe person to be around. Once I settled down and worked through it, thoughts like, "It's not a big deal, I'm making too much of this" would wash over me. Then, whoosh, I'd sweep my emotions back under the rug. It wasn't until I had kids that these bursts of anger seemed to come from nowhere. It felt like I was losing control of myself and becoming a completely different person. This was the aftermath of years of suppressing my emotions and betraying myself. It was a hard season of shaming myself, and my poor little boys were bearing the brunt of my childhood suppression.Understanding and being aware of past moments in our lives can help us extend grace for ourselves when we don't "get it right."

The risks that vulnerability exposes us to are real, but the rewards far outweigh them. Vulnerability is being honest with yourself and facing your pain. To face what hurt you and say to yourself, "My feelings matter, too." Being able to express our core emotions and actually share them with someone honestly is the heart of vulnerability.

I'm learning to love myself in the midst of being open. The only way to change old patterns of thinking is to face them and walk through them. Vulnerability has opened the door for me to understand myself. Being able to admit things like, "I don't feel safe when you do that," or as my husband and I like to say, "You hurt my heart." I can now recognize feelings when they come up and take a breath before I go into "react and attack" mode. It has been a challenge for me, and there are still times when I think I've got it all figured it out, just to find I've still a ways to go.

When my first album was coming out, I was trying to order some merchandise. My husband wanted me to create an account through this company so I could get a discount on my order. I had already spent a lot of time creating a sweatshirt and didn't want to go through the long process of signing up and recreating it. My husband was persistent though, so I did it. Normally, this wouldn't have been a big deal, however, because I did all the work the first time, I missed picking the right size sweatshirt when recreating, ending up with a small instead of a large. When I realized this, huge emotions of frustration and disappointment rushed over me, and I couldn't seem to shake them. These negative feelings only lifted when I was able to share with my husband that I was so upset with myself for being convinced to do something I really didn't want to do. Thankfully, he took responsibility and resolved the issue quickly. It has been in these moments where I don't understand why I can't shake things, that I realize I am suppressing myself and my feelings. The mess up wasn't the issue, it was not allowing myself to be heard that triggered such big emotions.

This can be the same with the Lord. If I think my thoughts are too dangerous for people, chances are I think they are too dangerous for God, too. But God is not a hurting human. He is love itself and knows everything about you. He knows what you are going to say before you think it. I don't know about you, but I would rather learn to share my thoughts with God so He can come in and walk through it with me than to pretend with Him and stay stuck.

Can it really be that simple?

When you can become honest and vulnerable with yourself, you will be honest and vulnerable with God, which, in turn, will spill over into your relationships. God will not punish you for being honest. He will not give you the silent treatment because He is mad at you. He will not walk away because your raw emotions aren't very Christian-like. God knows the courage it took to express those emotions and thoughts. He knows how to break through, reach us, and heal us if we are willing to take that step of courage and be honest and vulnerable with ourselves and Him.

Friend, you are so precious to Him. If God can use David after all he did and handle all of David's emotions written in the Psalms, still calling him a "man after God's own heart," He can and will handle yours with love and care.

Take the time in your Secret Place to be honest and vulnerable with God. Take a chance, be bold, be courageous, with Him. If you don't know where to begin, start with admitting that you're not always okay. Let it out, and say it out loud. Then invite God in. He has been waiting to help.

I Did Not See That Coming

Often, I have had to choose to either lean into the vulnerability I have learned with the Lord or retreat to the habit of running and hiding. This is when the hidden fruit of the Secret Place with Him is tested.

My husband and I had a miscarriage at the end of October 2020, and the baby didn't pass until Thanksgiving. The first three weeks were hard and painful. Denial stared me right in the face and never blinked once. Was it hope? I couldn't tell the difference at this point. I was looking for anything that would help me grieve this in a healthy way and keep my mind off of things. Acceptance was really hard for me, and I was exhausted at looking at all the blood every time I went to the bathroom, reminding me of what I had lost. I found myself trying to find solutions to heal faster, thinking I would get past the pain quicker, but now I know it was really a way to disconnect from the situation. I thought, *if I can just heal physically, then I don't have to keep feeling this pain emotionally.*

I did, however, find a book called *Finding Your New Normal* by Ray Leight. I read it to keep my mind off of what was going on inside me. Ray talked about how "it is okay to think all your thoughts," and how this religious way of thinking has affected most of us, causing us to think we can't be raw and real with the Lord about what we are truly feeling. You know, those thoughts that we quickly push aside, saying, "I can't think that." Those ugly thoughts that we ignore because we don't like that side of us or they surprise us because we didn't think that was in us. Yeah, those thoughts. I was keeping busy so I wouldn't be still long enough to see what those thoughts were. Those thoughts scared me to death!

Ray asked, "How can we take every thought captive and make it obedient to Christ if we won't allow ourselves to think our thoughts? How will we know what is a lie and what is truth if we keep pushing away those thoughts we think are too bad or too ugly to bring before the Lord? God cannot heal what we will not acknowledge."

I didn't want to admit that I was angry with the Lord over this miscarriage, thinking He had tricked me, but at the same time, I didn't want these feelings to get between me and the Lord. So, I booked a session with Ray over the phone.

I drove out to the countryside so I wouldn't be interrupted. Having three boys in the house can be very loud with little to no place to hide where they can't find you. As we started the session, I was hoping to go into the direction of healing my fear of rejection, but I just couldn't get past my anger toward the Lord. Everything inside of me just wanted to scream at God. That scared me! How could I be angry with the Lord? I felt like a child, throwing a tantrum in front of my father. It was hard. I've always felt that I can't be too honest or admit I'm struggling, and if I do and throw a tantrum *and* God blesses me, then shame would say, "You didn't have enough faith to trust Him." I also felt the Lord was quieter with me than ever before. Well-intentioned friends would tell me, "I just see Jesus sitting next to you," which frustrated me all the more! *Shouldn't God be doing more than just sitting with me and grieving?* Anger fueled questions like, "Why did you allow me to get pregnant, giving us all these confirmations and dreams just for us to lose the baby? I know I heard you clearly."

I doubted whether I could even hear His voice. I just didn't understand.

Something Big

In the beginning of 2020, a friend had shared a word the Lord had given her for me. "Something big is going to happen in your life, specifically to show God's amazing glory, and it will move you even closer to Him." I had assumed that word was for the same year it was given, causing me to keep a look out for this "something big." What could happen to bring Him glory and draw me closer to Him? By the end of the year, it felt more like a punishment. Although we didn't struggle like most people had during this tough year, our hopes for a new baby had been dashed. My thoughts were ugly. *Why would a good Father allow this to happen to me? Was it some kind of sick test?* As I sat there waiting for Jesus to respond with anger, what I got was nothing but love. Instead of, "How dare you?" I was met with Him holding out his hand for me to take. He didn't rush me to reach out. He didn't try to convince me. He just sat there in silence, waiting until I was ready. My hurt and unbelief didn't keep Him from being with me. He would wait for however long it took. I felt like one of those kids who acts mad and tries hard to stay mad, when really they just want to cry and be held. I knew the only way to get through this was to take His hand. I saw myself climb into His lap and fall apart. I just needed my daddy to hold me this whole time. I needed to feel loved by the One I thought caused me pain. A safe place to just cry. That's when I realized, Him sitting next to me was all I needed all along, and He knew it. He didn't want me to rush through this, but to sit and grieve properly. He wanted to draw me closer to His heart and be the One who sustained me through it all. He wanted me to know He was grieving with me and would walk with me through it.

During this time, not only did I realize the Father's goodness, but I also recognized that in all the time I spent with Him in the Secret Place, thinking nothing was changing, in reality, I was changing. I was able to be honest with Him in a way that I never had been before; my emotions weren't too big for Him, and He could handle anything.

I could face my pain *with Him*. The process of wrestling to trust Him with my heart and letting Him see into me, and then releasing control, being vulnerable with Him, was an amazing experience. I now became more vulnerable and honest with those closest to me. It's been the scariest and most freeing season of my life! Vulnerability is not easy. It's hard work, and it takes consistent intentionality, but in the end, it is worth every bit of courage I mustered, because it brought me closer to His heart.

Chapter 7

PRACTICAL STEPS

"We respond out of what we believe, not what we know."
—Ray Leight

Whole people help people. Whole people overflow. Whole people can stand in their identity while the opinions of others fall to the wayside. Whole people know how much they are loved by Jesus because they've allowed Him into their process and hurting places. Too many have been sold the lie that everything was taken care of at the cross and there is no process needed for that to truly happen. It is trials and tests that weed out and expose what we really believe and strengthen our faith. God was fully God and fully human when He died. When we come to Jesus in our sin, addictions, and faulty mindsets and say "the sinner's prayer," this doesn't mean everything will be fine in our life from that moment on. Sin won't just disappear, and healing won't always happen how we want it to. God requires us to play a part in life's journey with Him. This chapter reveals some human ways we can partner with God in our healing journey, both supernaturally and naturally.

Ownership

It's difficult to say, "This is my crap; I caused this," or "I was in the wrong; I'm sorry." The first step to ownership is being honest with yourself. Though the verdict is still out on whether people can "make" you feel anything it doesn't mean we invalidate people when they do have emotions and share them with us. I've learned and am still practicing when people come to me with their hurt feelings I can listen to understand and take ownership of my actions or words when needed or I can deny those feelings exist, pushing them off as "you being too sensitive or too emotional."

There are filters we use when we live in pain and rejection, known as *confirmation bias,* in which our mind will look for any and every sign of rejection to validate our pain. This keeps us stuck. Relationships struggle when we are subconsciously looking for rejection. A comment, a wrong tone, a seemingly irritated facial expression, all can seem like rejection when it's not. We are looking to confirm what we already believe is true.

How do we deal with this?

This is the tension I constantly live in!

This is why it is so important to have self-awareness. Knowing your triggers, learning to communicate through conflict, and avoiding detaching from a conversation in defense. You know, that part of the conversation when all you do is think about how you are going to respond. You are no longer listening but defending yourself. It took me some time to recognize this and what topics triggered my shame. My brain would go foggy, my hands and voice would shake, and I'd find it hard to speak. I now know this has nothing to do with the person talking or their opinion about the topic and everything to do with the shame that is attached to it.

So, what do I do when this happens? If I'm unable to express or understand what's happening to me, I remove myself from the conversation. If I don't, that's when I lay into someone and do the very thing to them that caused me pain in the first place. It's all done out of self-protection. That's a quick way to hurt a connection with someone. I've had to practice being self-aware, to identify where the trigger is coming from, ask myself questions, and to communicate them. Otherwise, instead of preventing messes, I have to clean them up more often than I'd like to (with much humility and apologies on my end).

The more aware we are, the easier it is to recognize our motives and gauge ourselves accordingly. Conflict becomes less personal.

Imagine if everyone had this level of awareness within themselves?

People have (and will) hurt you. You can either choose to live out of that pain or look it in the face and say, "You will no longer have control over my life." Your past has been coming to you saying, "I felt rejected, unloved, unvalued, belittled, not enough, like an inconvenience, unsafe, afraid…" It wants to connect with you and have you take the steps toward healing. If you continue to deny the past and its pain by pushing it aside as irrelevant, too much, or too emotional, it will leave you distant, disconnected, and still hurting.

To heal our past, we have to face our past.

Let's heal so we can stop accidentally hurting people we want to love.

Change

This requires action from us. Most of us have heard, "Actions speak louder than words."

Bill Johnson puts it this way: "Our words show us where we want to be, and our actions show us where we are."

Change is measurable. It's something you can see, revealed in our actions. It is frustrating to see another year pass by, and we are still stuck in that same old situation.

Maybe you haven't taken any action to change it. Maybe a negative belief has held you there. Thoughts like, *What if I start this thing and fail?* or *What if I can't do it?* Or maybe you don't think you are worthy of the success on the other side of your hard work. It's amazing how our actions point out our true beliefs. Change is a step-by-step process. It's those subtle changes we make every day.

Change comes in those moments your brain allows you to make a choice.

You know, those moments we respond without even thinking? An automatic reaction to whatever just happened. No thought, no process, nothing. It's a defense mechanism ingrained in you that has taught you how to act toward certain situations. Then there are those moments where our brain gives us that split second to make another choice. It's really quick and easy to miss.

I have had clear moments of choice. When my children are pushing me to the edge, I've thought, *Anna, you can either respond out of anger and yell, or you can take a deep breath and walk away until you can respond with love.* Change happens in those moments where we choose the behaviors we want in our lives. It seems so simple, yet not enough. But when we stay consistent in each little victory, eventually, we will look back and say, "Wow, I haven't freaked out on my kids in over a week" or "I haven't (you fill in the blank)." It's in the day-to-day, step-by-step moments that long-lasting change is made.

It's also important to recognize and celebrate all the small changes. It's easy to get frustrated when we don't see the big change happen quickly. Maybe we yelled five times this week instead of six. Focusing on where we fall short can be discouraging, but if we learn to celebrate every step of progress, I believe our frustrations wouldn't be screaming so loud and shining such a big light on where we are not at yet. By practicing this, we train ourselves to look for the gold instead of the dirt. And we might even enjoy the process a little more.

Responsibility

The dictionary defines responsibility as having a duty to deal with something, being accountable, acting independently, or having a requirement. To be trustworthy, powerful, or have authority.

"For those who have received a greater revelation from their master are required a greater obedience. And those who have been entrusted with great responsibility will be held more responsible to their master" (Luke 12:48).

When the Lord gives us revelation, we are now responsible to do something with it. When we choose to ignore it and not to use it for change, we are in sin. This is not to bring shame, but an enlightenment to the importance of our obedience. **Delayed obedience is still disobedience.** When God heals us, we are responsible to partner with Him in maintaining that healing. Whether that is by guarding our heart, watching what we hear and see, seeking accountability, or ending those activities that have opened a door to illness/injury. A higher standard is now required.

After my husband was set free from pornography, he downloaded an app that tracked everything he looked at on his phone. Each week, it sent me the results of suspicious activity. We also made a habit of heading up to bed together so the temptation at night was not there anymore. We would look up TV shows and movies before watching them so we would not get hit with any moral surprises. The point is, his healing came with the responsibility to protect it and not open doors on his end. To protect our hearts, we *have* to protect our eyes and our ears. What we watch and listen to has a direct effect on our heart. Maybe not the first time, but when we get that gut feeling about something, we can't ignore it. We cannot let those things that have caused so much pain and damage back into our lives, leading us down a road to something much worse.

It's been said marijuana is the gateway drug. This drug may be small in comparison to narcotics or ecstasy, but it opens the door to try more dangerous substances. We must fill up that space with the Lord and protect our healing with the authority He has given us.

What about when we've been shown that we struggle with gossip, slander, or a critical spirit? Gossip is an easy one for us, ladies, because we connect through spending time together and talking about everything. It's also an easy way to falsely connect with one another by pointing out the flaws in someone else instead of being vulnerable and talking about where we are struggling. When it is easier to talk about someone else's failures yet difficult to talk about our own, we are probably in avoidance or denial.

God's been highlighting to me jealousy and comparison. A stronghold with many women, which creates a false sense of connection and belonging. I hate it. The wrestle is real. Why is it so hard to celebrate others without comparing their progress with mine? The book of James says, "What is the cause of your conflicts and quarrels with each other? Doesn't the battle begin <u>inside of you</u> as you fight to have your own way and fulfill your own desires?" (James 4.1-4)

Wow! Our fight has nothing to do with each other and everything to do with lies we believe. The lies that say there isn't enough for both you *and* me. The lies that God is withholding something from me if you have it first. They keep us divided, against one other. These lies create pride within our hearts and make us think we are better than, because we actually feel less than. Isn't that crazy? The devil isn't stupid; there is a reason he is the accuser of the brethren. Yet, to hate a fellow believer is to be a murderer (1 John 3:15) and "Death and life in the power of the tongue" (Proverbs 18:21). Can we think about that for a second? Let's take this literally. First, there is death in the power of the tongue. Second, if you hate a believer, you are a murderer. Ladies, if we gossip, we've been cursing ourselves, bringing death, and keeping ourselves in bondage.

We've been made to believe that it's men who keep us stuck and keep us in bondage, but we've been walking around cursing each other and putting each other down with our gossip, our slander, and our critical spirit toward one another, ripping each other apart as if each other's blessing is the problem. Friend, imagine how powerful we could be together. What if we used our words to build up and not tear down? What if we focused on what change we wanted to see and put our energy into that, instead of being small and having that childish thinking that says, "If I can't have it, no one can."

Release Power with Our Words

Our words are supposed to release wisdom, empowerment, and support for one another. We have the power to bring healing and, through Christ, grace over people. We have the power to help break shame over peoples' lives, if we so choose. We have the power of life in our mouths, but we can't walk in love if we are too busy speaking death and killing people.

"But the tongue is not able to be tamed. It's fickle, unrestrained evil that spews out words full of toxic poison! We use our tongue to praise God our Father and then turn around and curse a person who was <u>made in His very image!</u> Out of the same mouth we pour our words of praise one minute and curse the next. My brothers and sisters, this should never be!" (James 3:8-18)

And you know what? I have been able to spew out toxic poison with the best of them. I have practiced taming my tongue through humbling myself by repenting and taking ownership through apologizing. If you want to start taking steps of action, then respond when the Holy Spirit convicts you.

Why not simply walk away from the conversation that you don't feel comfortable engaging in? Have you ever been in a conversation and felt so uncomfortable? Maybe you recognize the slander and gossip, but you don't know what to say or how to stop it, so you just stay silent, or you allow yourself to get sucked into it? I know I have. It's quite frustrating. I've noticed this in me, so I've learned there are people I just can't share things with because it quickly turns into "talking about" instead of talking to find a solution. There's a fine line between processing and gossiping. I've also learned to say things like, "That was a strange thing to say?" or "Have you talked to so and so about this?" One thing I'd love to say is, "If you don't talk to so and so by this time, I will." I don't know about you, but I want to be a peacemaker, not a peacekeeper. I don't want to ignore the "elephant" in the room for the sake of not rocking the boat. I want to be someone who can look pain right in the face and cut off gossip, slander, and criticism in its tracks.

Be Filled with Truth

Remember, to walk in truth, we have to fill ourselves with truth. Matthew 12:43-45 talks about casting out demons: "When a demon is cast out of a person, it roams around a dry region, looking for a place to rest, but never finds it. Then it says, I'll return to the house I moved out of, and so it goes back, only to find that the house is vacant, *warm,* and ready for it to move back in. So it goes looking for seven other demons more evil than itself, and they all enter together to live there. Then the person's condition becomes much worse than it was in the beginning."

I find it so interesting the verse says it's *still warm.* As if he wasn't gone long. Friends, know this, when you get free, the enemy will return to tempt you like in the garden. Did God really free you from that porn addiction? Are you truly free from alcohol? Come on, just have a taste. He will lie to you and say, see you're thinking about it, you're not actually healed from it. Do not fall for it! Friends, temptation IS NOT A SIN! Jesus was tempted in the desert for forty days. Temptation is the enemy's way of coming back harder than before. But I caution you, if you do not fill that space up with the Lord and His truth, you are leaving yourself *warm*, vulnerable to the enemy to prey on your weaknesses. This is why the word of God is so important, that we may read it aloud and build our faith by hearing the words God is speaking over us; that it may go deep within us, so on that day of temptation we will be able to stand and say, "No! I have filled this space with the Lord, I have been set free, you may not enter, leave right now!"

The Practical

So, why am I talking about practical daily steps? Because the Lord is practical, and He understands exactly where you are in life. He also wants us to know who we are and that He made us to embrace and believe this for ourselves. When we choose to surrender and follow God's leading, He will always lead us into discovery and healing because without it, we live life seeing through the filters of our pain, lies, and the strongholds we have built up in our minds. Healing is not an option when we choose to walk with God. It's also very important that we partner with what He is leading us into and revealing to us, otherwise, we can be overwhelmed, feeling solely responsible for our own healing. It is Him who heals, not us. Our job is to surrender and implement what He is asking us to in our daily lives, for He knows the healing we need today, tomorrow, and in every season.

This is so we can experience not only the "God of just enough," but also the God who is **more** than enough.

Chapter 8

OBEDIENCE

"I think that what separates us from our destiny and purpose God has for us, is our inability to continue to say yes to Him."
–Gabe Valenzuela

Have you ever noticed the silent yet "loud" push back when the word *obedience* comes up? How quickly it is ignored or met with a smile and nod as if to move past the topic quickly? It gets the same treatment as hard truth…nothing. I'm not sure this word is understood fully as it often has a negative vibe surrounding it. I believe obedience has been abused and used to bring manipulation and control over people and situations, commonly experienced through shame and embarrassment. I know this feeling well. For me, obedience meant. "You do what I say without any questions and you don't get a say in the matter." It also came with putting yourself out there so you could be embarrassed in front of a stranger in the name of, "Growing in hearing the voice of the Lord."

Love and relationship were not my experience. It caused much fear in me when I would feel the leading of the Lord to say or do something. This deep seeded lie rooted in me said, "God asks you to obey so He can make a spectacle of you." I realize now this is the furthest thing from the truth. Despite my deathly fear of obeying, it was still my heart's cry. I desperately wanted to obey the Lord with all my heart. I wanted simple obedience; I just didn't know how to take the first step.

When I look back through seven years of journals, I see this theme of *Radical love equals radical obedience*. I was so focused on the word *radical*. With this intense focus, I never realized how it was setting me up for disappointment in myself. When God would ask me to bless someone and I couldn't get myself to take that step, I'd beat myself up for allowing fear to win. But 2017 became my action year, the year that changed my life forever. My prayer became, *"to have SIMPLE obedience, to steward what you've given me well, and all for love."*

I know I've been so filled with hope differed that to hope and dream seems like wasted breath. But what happens when we do hope and it does happen? When I wrote that prayer down, God immediately took it and tested my seriousness. Six days later, I was worshiping at my piano when, out of nowhere, I heard, "Quit drinking." It was so clear, yet so subtle. It was as if the Lord was standing right behind me when I heard it.

I encourage you, do not shrug off that fleeting thought, as random as it might seem, but lean into it, write it down, and use it as an opportunity to start a conversation with the Lord.

I went back to the piano. I knew this was going to be hard. Alcohol was one of those "all or nothing" kind of things. I was either drunk or sober. There was no in-between. When life was hard or stressful, it was my go-to. It was normal for me to need some kind of substance to get me through instead of processing my emotions in a healthy way. I found myself relieved at this request though, because I had an excuse to stop. I was allowed to play the God card. I was also having an adult tantrum because we had just bought all the makings for Long Island iced teas (my all-time favorite at the time), and I would not be enjoying any of it. I would like you all to know though, I have not taken a sip since that moment. Well, okay, I took one sip. There was some in my husband's drink when I thought it was water. Oops. Surprisingly, to stop drinking was the easiest for me.

I was really worried it would be difficult to quit because many of the people around me still drank, including my husband. I have found when you have people who support and understand your decision, it helps carry the load. I was ready to let it go. Hearing it from God just made the choice easier for me. The Lord also asked me to lay down a TV show I was watching. Deep down, I knew it wasn't a good show, but, you know, I had nothing else to watch, so I just kept pressing play. I have now learned the importance of protecting my heart. If we continually consume media we know in our gut we shouldn't, it will eventually make its way in —and will eventually come out of us.

"So above all, guard the affections of your heart, for they affect all that you are. Pay attention to the welfare of your innermost being, for from there flows the wellspring of life" (Proverbs 4:23).

The third thing God had asked me to do was to give a dollar to a homeless person while I was with my girlfriends. Shockingly, I did not realize how much I cared what people thought of me. It was only a dollar, but it took me ten minutes to convince myself to do it.

I was walking up and down State Street in Madison, Wisconsin, at the time. State Street is over a mile long with restaurants and boutiques all up and down it. As we walked up the street, I saw a homeless man and heard God tell me to give him the money. I couldn't do it. I wrestled the whole walk up. Once we turned around, I knew it was now or disobedience. So, I swallowed my ego, discreetly took the money out, and slipped it into the man's cup. Now, it wasn't anything extravagant, but it was just that _simple obedience._ The last thing was to give money to a church during a conference. Spending money was hard for me. On top of that, I also had a spouse to think about when spending it. I was afraid of what he would think and whether he would see it as valuable.

I realize God really wanted me to trust Him no matter how it looked. I'm so thankful I said yes. Ever since then, my life has been a whirlwind. It hasn't been easy. At times, it has felt lonely and darn right horrible. But He has given me the opportunity to face my fears, to learn to become vulnerable, to be humbled, and to grow in trusting Him. Many times, I've wanted to give up, but I have learned it has always been worth it. The healing that has come is unmatched to the temporary pain or uncomfortable feelings I experience getting there.

Obedience is Heart Deep

When I think about obedience, I think about this question: "Which came first, the chicken or the egg?" We feel loved by the Lord and want to please him by obeying Him. But feeling loved by Him and loving Him are not the same. We see this in our inability to follow through when He asks something of us.

This started a beautiful dance of receiving and obeying between me and the Lord. My obedience once came from a hurting heart that wanted to prove I was a good daughter with an intense desire to fall in love at a deeper level with Him. I did love the Lord with all I could at the time. So, I obeyed Him at the level in which I loved Him. The Lord is so good to meet us where we are and uses what we have in our hands at that moment.

What I had in love to offer Him, He used and gave me little tasks that would encourage me and grow me, leading me to deeper love and trust with Him. With each step, He revealed more, and with each more, history between us was being built. I was falling in love with Him.

You can obey without love, but you cannot love Jesus without obedience. Jesus said, "Love the Lord your God with every passion of your heart, with all the energy of your being, and with every thought that is within you. This is the great and supreme commandment. And the second is like it in importance: You must love your friend in the same way you love yourself" (Matthew 22:37-39).

You see, to love God is to obey Him. To love yourself is to obey Him. To love your friend is to obey Him. Our obedience is a reflection of our love for Him. It reveals where our relationship stands and where there are lies. It is not to bring shame, but it is an invitation to go deeper with Him and to bring those broken thoughts about ourselves and His nature to Him.

Something I had to learn was, we don't obey for love, we obey because we are in love.

"Loving me empowers you to obey my commands" (John 14:15). The more I fell in love with Him, the more I wanted to obey Him. It is out of the overflow of our relationship with Jesus that we want to do what He has asks of us. It is out of our love for Him that the Fear of the Lord is displayed. John Bevere says it best, "The Fear of the Lord is not that we are afraid of Him but that we are afraid of being away from Him."

I have found that the one thing that will hinder our relationship and growth in the Lord is disobedience. Our disobedience ties the Father's hands in our lives. I'm not saying He ever stops pursuing us. We are His kids, and He always takes care of His kids. Choosing to disobey reveals something deeper behind our "no."

"This love means living in obedience to whatever God commands us" (2 John 1:6).

Could it be that we have made obedience this legalistic way of thinking, giving us an excuse not to? The Pharisees did everything the law told them to do. They fasted, they prayed, they memorized the Scriptures and could beat you to a pulp with them, yet Jesus called them vipers. Why? Because they chose religion over relationship and cared more about how they were perceived by man and didn't allow the voice of God to come in and deal with their hearts. It was about what they could do to prove themselves rather than being close to Him.

Obedience is Foundational

In Luke 6, Jesus explains how to build a house on a firm foundation. Jesus starts by asking, "What good does it do for you to say I am your Lord and Master if what I teach you is not put into practice?" I never truly saw this before until now. What good does it do us if we say God is Lord, read the word, and hear the Holy Spirit speak to us if we do not apply and practice what has been read or obey when the Holy Spirit asks us to do something? Jesus continues,

"Let me describe the one <u>who truly follows me</u> and does what I say. He is like a man who <u>chooses</u> the right place to build a house and then lays a <u>deep and secure foundation.</u> When the <u>storms and flood rage</u> against that house, it continues to <u>stand strong and unshakable</u> through the tempest, for it has been widely built on the right foundation. BUT the one who has heard my teaching but does not obey it is like a man who builds a house without laying a foundation whatsoever. When the storms and flood rage against that house, it will immediately collapse and become a total loss. Which of these builders will YOU be" (Luke 6:46-49).

Our foundation is in choosing to have an intimate relationship with Jesus, listening, and obeying when He speaks. Jesus is the living and spoken word that we follow and put into practice. Obedience is key in our relationship with Him. He strengthens us to withstand the storms, floods, and the tempests as we yield to his voice, surrendering ourselves. When we put action to our faith, it creates intimacy with our Lord. This has and will continue to change the course of our lives, and even of history (Hebrews 11). Obedience draws us to love Him more because we have experienced Him through our obedience, and it gives us strength and grace to do it all over again.

What if we stopped looking at obedience as a test we have to pass for God to find us worthy? What if it's the doorway to experiencing God's love in the way we've been longing for? "If someone claims, 'I have come to know God by experience,' yet doesn't keep God's commands, he is a phony and the truth finds no place in him" (1 John 2:4).

What if it is all about relationship and intimacy?

"But **the love of God will be perfected within the one who obeys God's Word.** We can be <u>sure</u> that we've truly come to live in *intimacy* with God, not just by saying, 'I am intimate with God,' but by walking in the footsteps of Jesus" (1 John 2:5-6).

Wow! God's love is perfected in us as we choose to obey Him. And when we fall short, it is an invitation to draw closer to Him and have a conversation as to what held us back from taking that step of obedience. What lie is holding us back from expressing our love to Him? It is really hard to follow someone we don't trust or we think will hurt us, yet so many of us want to experience the love of the Father, not realizing the lies we believe about Him are keeping us from putting action behind our faith.

Obedience Brings Revelation

It was November of 2017, and my husband and I were going on vacation with our best friends for the first time. Before the trip, I had a dream that a man bought a brand-new red sports car. Before he had driven his new car, he gave it to me to take on vacation. I woke up from that dream having no idea what it meant. The act in itself was so counterculture, it left me puzzled. All I knew was that whatever God was going to do, I was going to stand in awe of His goodness.

Wednesday morning into our trip, I was reading *Killing Kryptonite* by John Bevere in the three seasons room of the house we were renting. The end of each chapter featured an action statement, and this one read, "Invite Holy Spirit to have a conversation with you." Simple enough, right? In this season of my life, God was really honing in on obedience with me. I invited Him in, and I heard, "Go to the grocery store, find a man in all black, and tell him I love him."

I finished my time with Papa God and went inside. I ate breakfast, then just sat there. I was wrestling, trying to talk myself out of following God's guidance by questioning, "Was that really you, Holy Spirit? Do you really want me to do that? This is so hard for me." Coincidently, I happened to see to a video Stephany Gretzinger posted, of a spontaneous worship moment. She sang, "Sometimes my very best is only my weakest yes, <u>you see strength in every movement</u>." Instantly, I knew I had to do this. I mustered up the courage, then asked my husband, "Why do we struggle so much to do things God has asked us to do?" His response, "Because we doubt it's really Him." I said, "That's it! Well, I guess I'm going to go find out." I asked my husband to come along with me, and then everyone decided to tag along, too. No pressure there!

We arrived at the store. People were going in and out, but I just stood at the entrance, nervously watching for the man dressed in all black, secretly hoping he wouldn't show up. I saw many men wearing black, but some had white shoes or different color shorts. At seeing each one, my heart would jump into my throat! After some time, my friends were ready to go, yet there was still no sign of him. Relieved, I told my husband, "I need to look up and down the aisles just once before we go."

I couldn't walk away from that moment, knowing I didn't do all I could have to find him. Then I saw him, the man in all black, holding his child, standing next to his wife. I quickly told my husband, "Look, that's him!" Sheepishly, we walked down the aisle, slowly drawing closer. I was waiting for his wife to move away so I didn't seem crazy to more people than need be. Finally, he was standing by himself. I walked up to him and said, "Hi, this might sound crazy, but…" and went on to explain everything. As I was speaking, his face lit up, but he missed the part where I said, "God loves you." He asked,

"So, what's the word?" Stunned, I said, "That was the word; God loves you." Then I explained how hard this was for me to do. He responded, "Good for you, it pays to be obedient."

As we ended our conversation, I stood there in shock. Who says that? It pays to be *obedient*? We walked out of the store and told our friends what had happened. In the middle of retelling it, I started crying. I realized God did that for *me*. He did that to bless me, to give me confirmation and to say, "Good job, daughter." He wanted to break the mindset that He only asks us to speak to strangers to make fools out of us. Instead, He led me to who I believe was a Christian, to encourage ME. It wasn't even about the man in all black. It was about me! It was then I understood the meaning of my dream. I was in awe of His goodness.

"For I know the plans I have for you, says the Lord. They are plans for good and not for disaster, to give you a future and a hope" (Jeremiah 29:11).

If I wouldn't have said yes that day, I would have missed out on a blessing God had for me. One that rocked my world and caused a deep heart change. Friend, our obedience isn't just for those God wants to encounter through us but also for the transformation of our hearts and minds. Our obedience builds trust, shows where we haven't given Him full access to places in our hearts, uncovering the idols that still exist within, and reveals the lies we believe about His true nature.

Accept obedience is an invitation to go deeper with Him. To know Him is to experience Him, and obedience opens that door.

Trust

Obedience builds trust, but how do you build trust when you don't yet trust Him? It starts with taking the risk. Just doing it. Even when we find ourselves faced with fear.

What do we fear? That He won't come through when we muster up the courage to take that step of obedience?

What will happen if I say yes and do what I think He is asking of me, and it looks like it was all a waste of time?

What if we knew it was Him, had the confirmations to back it up, stepped out with big faith, and it all fell apart?
The question then is, is He still good?

Do we believe that God is good and loving, "Causing everything to work together for the good of those who love God and are called according to his purpose for them" (Romans 8:28).

Do we know the God of Scripture and believe what the Bible says about Him and about us? Do we believe it when it says, "But I have come to give you everything in abundance, more than you expect—life in its fullness until you overflow!" (John 10:10)

Do we trust in the God we have said yes to and have given our lives to by believing Jesus is our Lord and Savior? Or, do we only believe enough to get us into Heaven? Is that where it ends? On the contrary, this is where it was always meant to begin.

Obedience creates a history with God. It fine tunes our ability to hear His voice and the different ways it sounds. It leads us through the wonder and awe of Him as we watch Him put all the pieces together in a way we could have never imagined. We come to realize His ways are higher. I have a saying that goes, **"If I can think of it, then He probably won't do it that way."** Not that it can't happen that way. I truly believe God loves to show up in ways we never thought of to reveal how much He loves us and how child-like He really is in surprising us. It truly is a wonder to watch. If we want to grow, then obedience is key in that.

I challenge you to step out toward where you think God has been leading you. Let go of the worry that you may make the wrong choice. Beautiful friend, you are not that big. You are not that powerful to mess up God's plan for you and your life. Our fear of making the wrong decision is rooted in a deeper fear that is tied to a lie. For me, it was the fear of missing it or fear of punishment. A lie that He would withhold blessing from me or stop talking to me if I got it wrong.

His grace is too big for that. His love is too deep for that. He is too good for that! He is a good Father, and when it is time to change directions, He will tell you. Have you ever been on a walk with kids, and you told them to go straight at the stop sign but then changed your mind to go left or right? Do you just allow them to keep going straight while you turn? Or do you tell them to go right and keep telling them until they do? Even if they didn't hear you and continued to go straight, you would follow them until you caught up to tell them the new direction. You might grab their hand and say, "Hey, this way."

Friend, we do not need to worry, for our heavenly Father will never leave or forsake us. When we cast our cares on Him, even those reservations toward things we think He has asked us to do, He is so good to show us the way.

"Trust in the Lord completely, and do not rely on your own opinions. With all your heart rely on Him to guide you, and He will lead you in every decision you make. Become *intimate with Him in whatever you do,* and He will lead you wherever you go" (Proverbs 3:5).

Did you catch it? "Become intimate with Him in whatever you do." It all stems from this—everything we do in this life—from this one thing: intimacy with Him.

Chapter 9

ENDURANCE

"Letting go of control is to jump and risk to see if God is good."
–Marcus Miller[11]

Recently, I found myself getting triggered quite a bit. I knew it was time to sit down and address the thoughts attached to it. It came down to the lies of, "I'm not enough" and "Will it be worth it?"

When I think I'm not enough, it steals my joy from what God is doing at the moment. When I'm discouraged and ask myself, "Is it worth it?" what I'm really asking is, "God, are you worth following?" These lies distort things and shame me into thinking I am following God for the wrong reasons. This is the journey: discovering that I am seen and known by God, believing it takes time to heal, but with every step, lies are exposed, the truth comes in, and I learn to trust God even more.

Learning endurance has been a big part of my journey, and you don't learn that by getting what you want all the time and as fast as you want it. It's hard when I want things to move

---

[11] *Life consultant on Instagram*

quickly. I feel like I am not in control; that something is wrong with me, or that I am doing it all wrong. Then it's back to, "I must not be good enough." These are all thoughts I tell myself when there is no return for my efforts. It's exhausting, to be honest. Letting go and allowing myself to endure the process, resting in the confidence of who I am to Him.

Endurance is a dirty word nowadays. I understand why. It's hard; it challenges your will, your emotions, and your insecurities are exposed. It's an altogether downright sucky feeling. But we are told this will happen through trials and to be joyful because of what it produces in our lives.

"Even in times of trouble we have a joyful confidence, knowing that our pressures will develop in us patient endurance. And patient endurance will refine our character, and proven character leads us back to hope. And this hope is not a disappointing fantasy, because we can now experience the endless love of God cascading into our hearts through the Holy Spirit who lives in us!" (Romans 5:4-5)

I don't know about you, but trials don't feel joyful. They feel more like uncomfortable stretching I didn't ask for, or just didn't expect to look that way. All humans are wired to run away from pain. Makes sense, why would you keep running toward the very thing that hurts you? Sometimes the experiences that seem painful are actually refining us. To sit in the pain, in the silence of the unknown, not knowing how to fix things or which direction to go is hard. Feeling pain so I can actually heal? That does not feel normal, but very backwards.Wrong, in fact. Yet, these are the trials of life that require us to keep our eyes fixed on Jesus and mandate us to let go so we can let God work.

Often, trials are the only way to change our perspective. Our mind is renewed as we walk with Him in the stretching. Most times, He won't bail you out of it. His desire is to walk through it with you. If we are unwilling to walk through the storm or the fire with God, then we are losing the opportunity to be strengthened in Him. We run from the trial that produces the very thing we seek. If it were easy, everyone would be doing it. Endurance means showing up even when you've given your all to it, and still nothing seems to change. You keep giving your best continually and have seemingly nothing to show for it. Know this: the trials are creating character and endurance in your life. They were meant to lead you back to hope itself and to experience God walking with you in the midst, His love cascading over you every step of the way. God is not withholding from you, He is preparing you. And that's a hard truth to embrace when you come up against life circumstances that make you think otherwise.

The Waiting

You will be led into a season of waiting when walking with God. Waiting for promises fulfilled is a part of the journey you cannot bypass or control. I have found that the waiting can feel as if the Spirit has led you into the desert to be tempted, and with every opportunity to grasp ahold of your dreams, they just slip through your fingers. The test is getting victory over the lie that the Lord is withholding from you. You watch everyone else living their "best life" while you hang back, wondering what the heck God is doing with you. Jesus, too, was led into the wilderness, tested by the enemy, yet He stood on the word of God, speaking truth and standing firm in who He was and who His father was. The Holy Spirit didn't lead Jesus into the wilderness to punish Him but to "reveal his strength against the accuser" (Matt. 4). So the waiting will be with us. It is to build us up, not to tear us down.

If you are like me, you want to reach the end goal as fast as possible. You know, the part where the Scripture says Jesus came out of the wilderness with power. There isn't a transition hack in life you can use to skip over what God is trying to produce in you. It is produced by steps of trusting Him as you wait, wait, and wait some more. I wish more people shared about the struggles faced in the in-between. Showing us that they aren't some superhuman who can flawlessly handle it all but are triggered, have insecurities, and struggle, too.

Think about doubting Thomas. The poor guy was labeled for being honest with his process and being true with where he was at. As you read about this encounter in John 20, it says, "that one of the twelve wasn't present when Jesus appeared to them—it was Thomas." Now imagine you are Thomas. All of your friends have these amazing God stories about how He is moving in their lives, how they are stepping into their dreams. It seems like God is moving in everyone's life but yours. If you put yourself in Thomas's shoes, do you think you would have a little doubt, too? Everyone saw Jesus but you? What if his doubt was really him feeling left out and the demand to see Jesus himself was really a cry to be encountered?

Here is the best part: Jesus shows up eight days later by walking through a wall, speaking right to Thomas. Not only did He return just for Thomas, but He also made an unbelievable entrance. Jesus did not shame Thomas or punish him for doubting. Instead, He reveals Himself to the disciple in the midst of his doubt, instructing him to touch the wounds in His hands and side so he could see for himself. After encountering Thomas, Jesus says, "Don't give in to your doubt any longer, just believe" (Mark 5:36). Can I encourage you? If you are in a waiting season, lean in to Him, for He isn't upset or disappointed in your struggle. Rather, He is waiting for you to come to Him. He is committed to giving you the encounter your heart longs for.

This happened eight days later. Eight days can *seem* like a cake walk. But eight days inside of your head can also make you think something is wrong with you. Make you feel like you are missing out or you don't know what you did wrong. If this were me, I would be hashing it out with God in my mind and beating myself up trying to find answers. "God, why would you show up the one time I'm not there?" Our true beliefs are revealed in that moment.

When we think we have missed out, that God is keeping something from us, the spirit of lack speaks to us. "Where are God's promises now? He has forgotten you; abandoned you in this impossible situation. See? God isn't true to His word after all." These intense thoughts come to steal your trust in the Lord and create doubt in your mind.

The waiting is meant to build trust between you and the Lord. It feels like we have no control, not seeing its purpose. Our prayers become ultimatums. "I'll move when you tell me the purpose of my next step." What we are really saying is, "I don't trust you." Taking that first step often reveals the next step, and then the next one. This verse comes to mind: "Give God the right to direct your life, and as you trust Him along the way, you'll find He pulled it off perfectly" (Psalms 37:5).

My husband and I lived in a duplex for four years, and one day, our landlord announced he was selling the place. I was more than happy to move out, but it was slim pickings when it came to finding a place to live. I sensed we were in this transitional season, but it wasn't clear what we were transitioning into. I knew our next place would be short term, just a pit stop to where we were going next. My husband preferred the duplex life of not having anyone live above us upstairs. I asked the Lord if He would find a place where Joe didn't have to worry about it.

Now, my husband is the king at finding places and deals. He could book your whole vacation on a budget that would blow you away. Yet he had looked *everywhere* for a place for us to live, and nothing. I mean, he looked *everywhere.* We finally found this cute old house that was being turned into a duplex and because of the renovations, no one was living upstairs. The lease was only for nine months, so I took that as confirmation from God. It was just 900 square feet for all of us, but I didn't care. It was the cutest little cozy place, and I loved it, happy to be out of where we had been.

During those nine months, the Lord really did a lot in me. I was in that waiting process. You may be waiting for God to move. Some moves won't always make sense at the time, but they are all a part of a greater picture you will understand later.

The Lord spoke to me about a house. I don't know what thoughts come up when you think about owning a home, but mine were straight up NO! We had been married seven years and had moved three times. I was used to being mobile, knowing God liked to move us around a bit. The idea of owning a home and being planted somewhere scared the crap out of me. It made everything so permanent, and that was really hard for me. My sense of having control felt threatened. Not understanding why I was so resistant, I argued with the Lord for over a year on this.

When our nine months was up, we found ourselves in the same pickle as before. We couldn't find anything to rent or buy for the life of us. In desperation, I asked my mom if we could move in with her and Dad if we couldn't find a place Surprisingly, she said yes. I can still hear her excited, panicky scream on the other end of the phone when I called her to say, "We are moving in!"

It was a hot, humid day when we moved in with my parents. None of our friends were able to help us, and the one youth group kid who said he would help, slept through his alarm. My husband and I were left to pack, load, and clean the whole duplex by ourselves with two little boys. As easily as it could have been to have a poor attitude, we chose to hike up our britches and give it all we had with a thankful heart. To be honest, that was the easy part. Once we got to the storage unit, we had to unload in the heat, and I wasn't strong enough to do all this.

Thankfully, my dad came out to help us finish the unloading. There was no way we could have done it without him. When I look back on that day, I see the parallels of a good earthly and heavenly Father. When no one is around and you are left by yourself and can't carry the weight of it all, God always shows up. Just like my dad did that day. This was the beginning of a one-year journey of living with my parents as we trusted God to find our next place to live.

Stretching

Have you ever had to live with your parents through a transition? Let me tell you that once you've become independent, growing as your own person, moving back into your parents' house is like being a child all over again while simultaneously trying to be an adult to prove to them you grew up. Especially when you have kids of your own.

This four-bedroom home now housed four adults and two little boys, ages four and two. Tensions grew as two new millennial parents stumbled their way into a parenting style that fit them as their baby boomer parents watched, scratching their heads. I heard a lot about parenting during this time. I had also given birth to the strongest-willed child I ever did know. My four-year-old once chose to sit on a soft plush rocking chair for four hours because he refused to read that day. It was a challenge to stay consistent. It got so hard for me, I had to hire someone to help me parent my boys.

I had arranged a free fifteen-minute call with Seth Dahl, from Spirit-led Families Ministries. The second I started speaking, I broke down crying. I felt so powerless as a mother. Through our short conversation, we discovered the power struggle I was having with my first born. Again, I was met with this need for control, and it was being stripped from me. We all want to be perceived as good parents, but parenting is messier than I would like to admit. Blood, sweet, and tears is no joke as a parent. I have learned that endurance knocks on your door when you are faced with trials, and the choice is either to change or stay the same.

I think it's safe to say most of us do not enjoy trials. We don't like being in situations that bring pressure. However, it's how we grow. So how do you keep moving forward when you feel like you're barely surviving? For me, I had to be vulnerable with my husband and let him know I was exhausted, felt defeated, and most importantly, I needed help. That was a big one. How many of us ask for help when going through a hard time?

When we began working with Seth, we had to learn new skills and vocabulary in dealing with our kids. We had to give them choices instead of just telling them what to do; and when they resisted, we had to learn to exercise patience and not get mad at them. They had to learn that their choices, whether good or bad, have consequences.

Ultimately, we learned to let go of control and be consistent people of our words.

It wasn't easy, and it took a lot of hard work. We missed many date nights, but through time and many choices, we started to see change, and life wasn't so unbearable with our kids.

These were the dynamics we dealt with for nearly a year—navigating parenthood, trying to find a home, and doing our best to honor and respect my parents' house rules. We were stretched immensely. With the pressures of it all, it would have been easy to settle for an Ishmael.

Wait or Create?

An Ishmael starts looking good when the waiting has been challenging and the process takes longer than expected. Doubt sets in. Will God's promise ever come to fruition? (Gen. 16:1)

One way the Lord speaks to me is through dreams, especially during transition periods. He is faithful to direct me to the next thing. My husband and I had looked at this house that reminded me of a place I'd lived in when I was eight. I had so many fond memories of the "Elsie Street House." When we walked through the door, I instantly noticed a big, beautiful fireplace made of stone—nearly identical to the fireplace in my childhood home. All of these warm, fuzzy feelings came over me, and I envisioned all we could do in this house. The downside was the basement needed remodeling, and we had no idea the kind of work needed to be done. I was set on buying it, but then I had a dream. My husband was about to close the deal, and as we went to sign the papers, I heard the Lord say, "Don't buy the house." I quickly ran over to my husband shouting, "Don't sign the papers; God says this isn't our house." So, we didn't buy it.

In my experience, while waiting for dreams to come to pass, opportunities to doubt God arise. We want to take things into our own hands and settle for less than God's best. We think, *this must be what I've been waiting for.* Trust Him. Be willing to lay that down, knowing He has the best for you.

God doesn't give us crap to teach us a lesson. While we were on our house hunt, we found a duplex. From the outside, it looked so cute and had a fenced backyard. That was important to me since we had the boys *and* a dog. We walked in, but an overwheling dread suddenly came over me. Everything about it reminded me of where we used to live. I battled with the idea that God would bring us right back to what we left in the name of obedience. I felt used, that I didn't have a say, that what I wanted didn't matter. I realized then I had faced the opportunity to choose to go back to where I came from, go back to the comforts of my past, OR I could embrace all the closed doors and make good use of the time I had with my parents and all the beautiful things that came with that. God's best often looks like inconvenience when really, it's a blessing in disguise. My boys spent a whole year with their grandparents, allowing my husband and I to go on weekly date nights and worship nights at church. If that wasn't enough, we were able to save enough money for a down payment because we didn't have to pay rent. I made dinner for everyone three nights a week on the days my parents worked, and we all ate together. Pretty sweet deal, if you ask me. We grew closer to each other and stronger spiritually through it all.

The Promise was Waiting

"Hope deferred makes the heart sick, but a desire fulfilled is a tree of life" (Proverbs 13:12).

Spring was around the corner. Our oldest boy turned five, and I was now pregnant with our third child. We were getting antsy, and with no home in sight, the desire to have our privacy back only increased the pressure to find a home. We went to every open house and found a realtor to help us. It was a busy spring.

I had found one house online, but the pictures, especially of the kitchen, were not appealing. Later, my mom was looking and found the same house. I said, "Nope." Then, my husband saw this same house! Again, I was completely against it, but my husband really liked it, so we booked a time with our realtor to go check it out. I was glad we saw it in person because the photos did not do it justice. We both liked it, but it was out of our price range, even though they reduced the asking price by ten grand.

We left the showing, got some ice cream, and talked about it. Emotions were in the air.

That night, I had a dream. I was walking past a man I knew was prophetic when he turned to me and said, "Congratulations on your new house." I was hesitant to receive this word, as it wasn't official yet. That was it. I woke up and told my husband the dream and said, "Let's make an offer." We countered with the highest we could. They dropped the price another ten thousand. We offered five thousand more and bought the house for twenty thousand less than their original asking price! Here is the kicker. My grandma told me multiple times through this process, "Anna, if it's for you, then it will be yours." She was right. I had said no to this house three times, and yet God kept bringing it up. God knows how to get through to us. This house sat on the market for four months when the housing market was crazy. It was like God saved it just for us.

Looking Back

After we had moved into our little miracle home, I realized all the ways God answered our prayers. It left me in tears for months. Little things like having a kitchen window facing the backyard so I could do dishes while watching my kiddos. He gave me an open concept house with an island in the kitchen and first floor laundry. We had a fenced in backyard, a park down the road, and were half a mile away from a bike trail.

All these things were important to me. My husband wanted a finished basement with a built-in bar so he could host our friends during the Super Bowl or fantasy football. We now lived just seven minutes from friends and family. Our home has been filled with people and laughter ever since!

After a decade of not having a place to call my home, God made a way. Without that time at my parents, it wouldn't have been possible.

Hindsight is always twenty-twenty vision to enable us to say, "Wow, God, you took care of us and pulled it off perfectly." Yet, in the moment, all we can see and feel is the struggle, the lack, the pressure, the conflict, and the inconvenience of it all. *How* we wait does matter. It's okay to have big feelings and talk it out with the Lord. But make sure you are obeying while you do it. There is always a purpose for His request to wait. He does not waste anything. If we are willing to trust Him through it all, even when we want to quit, even when we want to settle, and even when it seems hopeless and like it will never happen, we will be rewarded with His best.

"Don't get weary in doing good, for the harvest is near if you do not give up" (Galatians 6:9).

Chapter 10

THE WILDERNESS

"You can't expect God results without a God process."
–Shawn Bolz[12]

Now that we have said yes to the process, chose to follow His leading through obedience and are willing to be stretched, we may find ourselves, from time to time, in a transitional season known as the wilderness. Some call it the hallway, while others call it the unknown. Whatever you may call it, you can bank on going through one at some point in your life.

The wilderness feels like limbo. Learning to live in the tension of doing the day-to-day while maintaining the expectancy of change. You may not know what you are building toward, but you consistently steward what God has given you to do, obeying even when it doesn't look like it's building toward your dreams. It feels mundane, never ending. Weeks turn into months and sometimes years. You wonder if God forgot about you. It's here you learn to celebrate others in their blessings, supporting them by listening or cheering them on.

---

[12] *Shawn Bolz is a TV host, author, producer, and prophetic minister.*

The wilderness is where you think you are going to die but actually come alive. Where trials come to take you out, but you learn you have authority in Jesus's victory; where you thought it was the end but instead, you come out with resurrection power and oil. The wilderness builds your strength in the Lord because you've learned that your boldness and persistence in self has been stripped and refined into boldness of faith and humility that only comes from His strength. In the wilderness, everything you hold dearly is asked to be released so you can let go of how you think it should be and trust Jesus with everything. Nothing else defines you, only the One standing in front of you. The Audience of One is being restored in you. It's where you meet Jesus face to face.

The Unknown of You

My wilderness experience was about following God into the "unknown of me." The unknown is your potential, the version of yourself you daydream about; the you that lies on the other side of your fear, the you God has always known from the beginning. The you who needed the process of building confidence and trusting Him along the way.

The wilderness taught me that I put my identity in who I could be for God and how that looked in the sight of men. This revelation came through constantly surrendering my ideas, my timing, and the expectations of my dreams. The wrestle of "letting go and letting God" is real, revealing what we are still hanging on to. When God brought me into the wilderness, I thought it was because of some much-needed rest. Yet the longer I stayed, the more restless I became. I saw all the opportunities for my dreams to be realized fall away. It crushed me. When I embraced the process and the waiting that was attached to it, I felt I was losing me. I desperately attempted to fix it, hoping the pain of the season would bypass me. This wasn't a month-long learning process. No, seven years and a painfully slow realization that He brought me to the wilderness to heal my heart, to reveal to me who He was. He stripped everything away that kept me from His love. He taught me how to receive and to accept me for me, embracing His reality so I could step into my identity. It was always about His love for me, and it took a long time for me to stop looking at the storm around me and to focus on the eyes in front of me.

I've always had a strong need to obey the Lord, to prove myself and be seen. When God asked me to do something, with everything I could muster, I would do it. Even when my motives weren't pure. Yet, without realizing it, when God asked me to do certain things I would think, *God must be asking me to do this because I'm going to be successful in it.* Of course, this would lead to disappointment when things didn't work out that way. The stripping and transforming of my mind then began.

In the wilderness, we will face our fears, but God does everything with the intention to pull us closer to His love, to draw out what He sees in each one of us. The big moments of breakthrough and revelation in our lives is not when we finally think we've "made it," but in the everyday moments of constantly saying yes and finding fresh eyes for Jesus every day.

The wilderness will look different for everyone. This is what mine looked like.

My Journey

As I mentioned previously, 2017 was my action year. I had decided to become a Beachbody Coach. Beachbody is a company that creates home workout programs and offers supplements such as protein shakes and much more. You basically exercise for a living. Choosing to be a coach would pull me out of my comfort zone. It involved recording yourself working out, putting yourself out there in hopes of encouraging others to join you. I've never liked the idea of cold calls, so I really struggled getting clients. I'm normally a goofy person in front of the camera, but when I feel uncomfortable, I get really serious and robotic or get so goofy I can't get through a sentence without laughing. The whole process was so uncomfortable, especially being vulnerable in my recorded workouts, showing people my struggle, my sweat, and long progress toward getting healthy again. I thought I was going to make so much money, after all, I thought God had led me to do this. I committed to one year, and I stuck to it. Financially, I was successful for the first four months, then fell flat on my face. That wasn't helpful for my ego. God eventually blessed me in the end, but what I was expecting to happen, didn't. I learned that the process takes time. It takes showing up every day, even when you don't see results. It looks great when you see the before and after pictures, but there is a lot in between. That is the process. And it takes showing up, doing the work no matter what you see. This is what the wilderness is like. Learning to accept yourself in every stage of the process and letting go of the destination, embracing each day as it comes.

The following year was my "just do it" year. More of saying yes to things I didn't want to do. One of these was starting a blog. God had asked me to start one in 2017, and it took some time, but with the constant encouragement and help from a friend, I was able to get it up and running. Again, I thought, *Oh, God must be asking me to do this because I'm going to reach so many people.* I laugh at myself when I think about that and marvel at the goodness of the Lord. He knows our thoughts and insecurities. He also knows our hidden motives, even when we don't, and still chooses us.

Unsure what I would be writing in these blogs, I shared things God was showing me, thoughts about my daily process, and anything else I was pondering.

I was always looking for approval from those close to me, gauging what I did for God by their acceptance of it. I hid behind the fear of misrepresenting God, getting the meaning of Scripture wrong. I was fueled by being right more than stepping out in faith and learning. It didn't help that I never got much response on most of my blogs. God wasn't using it for others but to pull something out of me that HE saw as valuable. I had spent years writing in many journals, and now He was bringing it out to small, bite-size pieces. If you had asked me what God was doing with me through this blog, I would not have had an answer for you. I didn't know because I couldn't see the bigger picture. I could only see in the moment and what I wanted Him to do with it.

My year of "acceleration and fruitfulness" was 2019—I was *all in*. This year was a mixture of transitions and focused on consistency and doing my best to thrive by doing things well. We also began going to a new church and joined five other couples to worship once a week. This was also the year we moved in with my parents. We weren't expecting a new job for my husband that would change everything for us, in a good way. We moved into our "God-chosen home" and welcomed a new baby boy. It was an eventful year, and we were just practicing showing up during all the transitions.

I noticed the growth in me when it came to being present and enjoying the stillness. I didn't mind the late nights with the baby and enjoyed just sitting and holding him. I loved not feeling like

I had to rush off and do something. I soaked it all in, and that changed everything for me.

The year 2020, the same "something big" year, was also to be my "stronger" year. I think it was everyone's year to build strength as we all discovered our true foundations. We trusted God to protect us, still do life, and for my husband and I, we banded together with friends and worshiped corporately, despite the crazy that was the world at the time.

This would also be the year my husband and I started our farmhouse sign business.

God asked me to take on the social media world once again. Opening my Facebook page, I was overcome by fear. I reached out to my best friend for support and heard some much-needed truth as she held my hand virtually and helped me embark on that new adventure. I would encourage, edify, and empower women in the Lord in this journey of loving ourselves through the process. I did this by sharing real struggles and how God brought light to the lies I believed. This required me to go live on my social media pages. And how nerve-racking this was for me! I'd set up my notes and for fifteen or twenty minutes before going live, I'd just stare at my phone, looking for any excuse *not* to press that live button. I was terrified! This weird mind game began where I would be disappointed if no one was on my live feed, but the second anyone would join, my face became flush, and nerves washed all over me. I would lose my train of thought and stumble in my words. If someone made a comment, that was it! I would lose my place in whatever direction I was going. It was an awful learning experience.

What is it about that live button? Is it the vulnerability of the story? The hope for validation and man's approval? Why does that little square box we carry around with us every day cause so much fear? That was my challenge for the year, to show and share vulnerable moments. God valued my voice. This caused me to do it afraid and with each yes, little by little, I gained confidence. I had to learn that just because you aren't seen, it doesn't mean you aren't valuable. If God said it, then it must be true, so believe it.

Again, it's this idea of showing up for yourself. How many of us do things for the results instead of for the sheer enjoyment of it? God's process for me has been interesting, and with each step comes breakthrough, and every yes of obedience, more revelation of His ways.

Now in 2021, God spoke sonship to me. My best friend was given a book by Chad Norris called *Mama Jane's Secret*. This book wrecked me, opening up encounters with the Father in ways that changed my relationship with Him forever. So much about the word of God is believing what He thinks about us as truth. We can be in Christ yet live as an orphan every day of our lives. How is that possible? Because it's not enough to just believe in Jesus as our savior. There is so much more for us than our salvation. We were put on this planet to dwell as sons and daughters of the Most High. See like Him, walk like Him, talk like Him, and live life knowing we are completely loved by the Father, that we have authority in Jesus over disease, death, and the grave. Jesus gave his last breath so we could live again. How can we walk into everything God has for us when we won't see ourselves like He does? We were made to experience Him.

I used to get so frustrated when people said our identity is in Christ. Okay, but how do you do that? We need a revelation of what Jesus did for us.

I was worshiping one morning, singing how Jesus knew what He was saying yes to when He went to the cross, and I heard the words, "I do." Jesus still gave His last breath so we could live again, knowing we would have an affair with the things of the world over Him. Though salvation was enough, He still got down on one knee, asking, "Will you marry me, church?" He promised to never leave or divorce us. And when we fall short, Jesus intercedes for our victory. He never gives up.

I wonder if this is why it is difficult to watch the movie, *The Passion of the Christ*, or if we do, we don't watch it more than once. It's hard to handle, to acknowledge that someone would go through such pain because of their great love for us. Yet, for us to understand identity and sonship, we need a revelation of what Jesus did for us. We have to know the cost of His sacrifice on that cross. It is foundational. From there, we can now believe we don't have to work to sit at His table. We don't have to prove ourselves. He proved His love is true and is not going away; it has been tested and approved.

This is what came out of me as I learned to embrace identity, not just knowing it with my mind but with my heart and my very being.

"Intimacy is growing deeper. A knowing is starting to settle in. Sons and daughters standing, knowing who He is. His love washing over them, cascading. He surrounds them. They know His heartbeat because they lay their head on His chest listening. Resting on Him as he breathes, slowly they sync. Breathing in and out with Him. This is identity. This is knowing, this is kingdom living. This is what it looks like to be His children."

The year 2022 was my "advance forward" year. God spoke to me about being bold and courageous; not to grow weary in doing good because of the harvest I'd reap if I didn't give up (Gal. 6:9). God reminded me of the Israelites wandering in the desert. Transition is a test and a time to learn and grow (Hebrews 3:8-10). Our unbelief can breed sin and disobedience.

"They grieved God for forty years by sinning in their unbelief, until they dropped dead in the desert...they would never enter into his calming place of rest all because they disobeyed Him. It is clear that they could not enter into their inheritance because they wrapped their hearts in unbelief" (Hebrews 3:17-19).

Sin is rooted in what we believe about ourselves and God, and it is impossible to move forward in what He has for us and to stand in who He says we are when we won't believe what He speaks as truth. Amazingly, God still provided mana and what they needed for each day, despite their unbelief, for God always takes care of His children. God knew that, to get the "Egypt thinking" out of them, they needed to go through this process.

Could it be that unbelief keeps us only knowing the God of enough, but belief introduces us to the God who is more than enough?

This was the year of crossing over into my promised land. I gained direction with my music and practical steps to make things happen. God had something in mind. This would be a year my husband and I would turn inward toward each other and pour into our family. Codependency would be broken off of me. This was something that needed to shift in me for so long. I needed to learn to trust myself and the voice of God within me. I had always looked for validation from others over God's approval. It was a time of intense focus, personally, to do the two things God had asked of me: finish this book and write music. Like King David, God would give me a strategy to overcome and walk in victory. He will do it for you, too.

20/20 Vision

I found that my journaling led to blogging, which led to writing this book.

Putting myself out there with Beachbody on social media led to going live on Facebook and Instagram, provided encouraging talks on TikTok, which eventually led my fear of man being stripped away. Moreover, I had a newfound value of my voice and what God had deposited in me.

God will always lead you to where He needs you to be. He will highlight a person, a podcast, a course you need to take, igniting a desire to learn more. He creates desires in you so that you will seek them out.

While taking a course in June of 2021, I made a friend who encouraged me and eventually connected me to my now publisher. She, too, was writing a book and found this amazing publishing company that worked with charismatic Christians.

This would lead me on a journey of being prophesied over by this publisher and of stepping out in faith and obedience. My publisher, Sherry, and I worked on my mission statement, and as I read it aloud, I broke down crying. I couldn't begin to say how true it was! My spirit connected with these words, and tears of joy flowed out. God named things within me that I have been searching for my whole life. It has taken 33 years to get me to this point. But here I am.

Friendship with the Lord takes time. Lots and lots of time. By throwing away the mindset of a time limit, we are free to enjoy the process with Him even more. Friendship looks like life. Be attentive to when God is speaking, and follow His voice.

If God had never challenged me and I never took those steps of obedience, this book would not have been written. God loved on me, broke through false mindsets, and addressed the lies within me. Even if God drawing me to write this was just to heal me, it would have been worth it. But I know when healing comes, we overflow with a little more love and can meet others in their struggle. It's easy to think it's about others first, but it is YOU He longs to restore first. He wants *you* to thrive just as much as you want others to thrive. But He won't do it at your expense. And you can't lead others where you haven't tread yourself.

Everything I sought and longed to become was already there. I just couldn't see it because I didn't believe in me. God saw it the whole time and was pulling it out and refining it. He is saying, "See, baby girl, this whole time you were walking in it. We have been walking this journey together. You've been allowing Me to refine your message by allowing Me to love on you where you were at, and step-by-step, we grew together. You allowed Me to love you deeper, and you trusted Me more; you've embraced and loved yourself as I love you. I *was* answering your prayers, moving in your life in extraordinary ways. It was a step-by-step process of learning to trust me in the day-to-day."

Chapter 11

STAND IN THE KNOWING

"I know Him, and I would be a liar, like yourselves, if I told you anything less than that" (John 8:55).

It all comes down to learning who you are in Him. Saying yes to the process and walking in truth. You will hold your head high and stand taller. You will recognize lies quicker and run to Jesus for His truth more often. You will Stand in the Knowing of who the Father says you are. You will emerge confident as a daughter of God. Authority will follow your breakthrough—and hell has no power over a child who knows the truth, the power of Christ in her.

Jesus understood this. In the Scripture above, Jesus was responding to Jewish leaders who had accused Him of thinking He was greater than He was. Hell will question you, "Who do you think you are?" But we are not those who are held back by fear and shrink back. Jesus knew who He was and boldly spoke it and lived it. He knew His Father loved and accepted Him, and because of this, He would not settle for believing anything less than who His Father said He was.

You have permission to stand in God's truth. The truth in His word and His word spoken over you. You have permission to stop living like a worthless sinner who doesn't deserve the scraps off the table. And you have permission to believe that you are a child of God who stands at the right hand of the Father, fully accepted, because Jesus gave His life for you to stand there with Him! Your identity is not in sin, your identity is in Christ!

"Give me more revelation so that I can live for you, for nothing is more pure and eternal than your truth!" (Psalms 119:144)

There is a kingdom inside of you. It is the gift of Jesus, the love of the Father over you. It's the Holy Spirit flowing out of you. It is the Great I Am in you! When Jesus said, "On Earth as it is in Heaven…" He was thinking of you! From the beginning of time, He had a dream, and it came to life when He thought of you.

> Believe that…
> You are His.
> You are loved.
> You are chosen.
> You are precious.
> He will never leave you or forget you.
> You are worthy.
> You are enough.
> You are favored.

You are not alone.
You are set apart for His glory.
You are His, and He is yours.
You are because He IS!

He will love you until the end of time, and that is never ending.

Will you choose to believe His reality over you?

"If you really knew God, you would listen, receive and respond with faith to his words" (John 8:47).

This is why we embrace the process and do the inner work because if we do not know the truth, then we will not recognize lies when they come. This is why we learn to listen when He speaks truth over us, then receive that truth and respond in belief to what He has spoken. The time has come for us to stop believing only enough to get us to heaven, but not enough to see heaven on earth. John 8 goes on to say that when we do not listen and respond, it is because we have no room for Him in our hearts. You see, the devil wants you to believe there is no hope for you. This is not the case with us; we do have hope.

"*If God has determined to stand with us*, tell me who then could ever stand against us? For God has proved His love by giving us His greatest treasure, the gift of his son" (Romans 8:31).

Did you catch it? God is determined!

Determined

1. having made a firm decision and being resolved not to change it.

He is calling you and speaking His reality over you. He has not changed His mind about you and will never change His mind about you. He will continually speak into who you are. If you haven't seen the TV series, *The Chosen,* I encourage you to watch it. In one episode, Jesus meets a boy named Joshua who is acting shy, but Jesus continues to speak to his true identity every time He sees him, saying, "Joshua, the Brave!" This is how Jesus speaks to us. No matter where we are in life, He is always calling us by what *He* sees.

Know Truth

"For if you embrace the truth, it will release more freedom into your lives" (John 8:31).

What does it look like to embrace truth?

Embrace
1.   to hold closely (as in one's arms) a sign of affection
2.   an act of support, acceptance, belief

To embrace implies a willingness and enthusiasm. Most people spend their time running from the truth. They actually fear what can set them free. Embracing truth requires acknowledging, taking ownership, changing, and taking responsibility. Allowing Jesus into our hearts to shed light on those hurting places suffocated by lies requires emptying ourselves, being vulnerable, humble, and obedient.

If you are anything like me, the kind of person who just wants to know the steps I need to take so I can move through this as fast as possible, you want to hurry up and move forward. But there is no "one, two, three, now I'm free" steps. It's all rooted in relationship. It's the following of the Holy Spirit to explore and discover what He is showing us, and it will look different for everyone.

"God conceals the revelation of His word in the hiding place of His glory, but the honor of kings is revealed by how they thoroughly search out the deeper meaning of all that God says" (Proverbs 25:2).

We are those kings, and the searching is to draw us closer to love. But we need discernment to know what is for us and what is not for us in each season.

Ephesians 3:20 adds to this as God desires to go beyond what we hope to find when we seek Him. "Never doubt God's mighty power to work in you and accomplish all this. He will achieve infinitely more than your greatest request, your most unbelievable dream, and exceed your wildest imagination."

It brings God joy to reveal Himself to us. But believing this is key.

"Then, by constantly using your faith, the life of Christ will be released deep inside you, and the resting place of his love will become the very **source** and **root** of your life" (Ephesians 3:17).

When we use our faith, which is believing and trusting God, the life of Christ is released inside us, and God's love becomes the very source and root of our lives.

"Then you will be empowered to <u>discover</u> what every holy one experiences—the great magnitude of the astonishing love of Christ in all its dimension. How **deeply** <u>intimate</u> and far-reaching is His love! Endless love beyond measurements that transcends our understanding—this **extravagant** love pours into you until you are filled to overflowing with the fullness of God!— NEVER DOUBT..." (Ephesians 3:18-19).

We were made to discover and experience His love. It is what grounds us. It is the reason we are here. It is what gives us our Godfidence as daughters and sons of the King. Trust that He will fulfill more than your greatest request!

Know that even though we are close to Him, He wants us closer still. Do not worry about tomorrow, be with Him today.

Do you believe His reality over your life?

I know I did not, and it's something I am still learning to embrace in my life. I'm learning to Stand in the Knowing. I am leaning into Him and who He says I am. I want to stand in every word that He has spoken, every yes and amen, every promise given! To deny who He says I am would be to deny my very being. Friends, when we deny and choose not to believe who He says we are, we are denying Him. When God reveals truth to us, it is our responsibility to stand in that newfound truth. Sometimes, it is as simple as saying, "God, I hear you saying this about me, but I don't yet believe it. Help me with my unbelief." Then, continue to speak what God spoke over you until you believe it.

Let's say some thoughts come to you saying you aren't enough. Stand against that lie and say, "I am a child of God who is accepted and adopted by Abba Father, and He says by His spirit I no longer have to live in fear of never being enough, for I am now family and fully accepted by Him." *This* is standing in the truth that has been revealed to you and choosing to believe in it. You declare it and speak it out every time lies come to tell you the opposite of what God has promised you. When you are unsure, come to the Father and ask what His truth is over you. Practice allowing His words to speak into our identity from His perspective. We are learning to rewire our thoughts.

Trust Him with all of your being, even when your heart is hesitant and doubt tries to creep in. Will we choose to listen, receive, and respond despite what our feelings are saying? Will we choose to be honest with our thoughts, no matter how ugly? Because, friends, our hearts do not scare Him but instead draw us to Him. He already knows the lies that entrap us and keep us from moving forward in His love and truth. He has the answer, He knows the way! He is the truth that will set us free. If only we would respond to the drawing that is His voice to reveal the lie so that He may speak the truth into our hearts and believe it with our minds. Stand in the Knowing of who He says we are.

You Have What You Need

'Today is the day you get to make a decision, either you agree with how I see you or keep living insecure." - Jason Clark

As I have shared before, my strength and weakness is my need to "figure it all out." I want to know what's next, how things will turn out, and if I'm doing it right. What I've realized is, when I feel out of control, my need to figure it out goes to the next level. Since April of 2022, God has led me to release my first album. It's a dream come true, and as the release of my first song gets closer, I started to feel out of control without fully realizing it. I began seeking for what was "next." I did this by asking my close friends if they would ask God for a prophetic or encouraging word for me for my birthday. Although there is nothing wrong with this, I was stepping into striving and out of trusting and resting in God. How does this tie into Standing in the Knowing of who I am? My mind was thinking, "With my luck, God won't give anyone anything." My heart, however, was just not content with what was already given. You see, I have a journal with a ton of encouraging words I've received from just this past year. More than I've received in many years. Yet, what was given wasn't what I was looking for. I was looking for a path and a future lit up with clarity, but God was giving me light shining on each step as they need to be taken. This frustrated me, as I want to have it "all figured out." This is where God continues to gently remind me of who I am. He did, indeed, give one of my friends a word for me for my birthday; it was just what I needed.

"It's time to lay down the 'scavenger' hunt for it's time for the 'treasure hunt.'" This is how my birthday word started out. It hit me so hard as my friend spoke this over me. I had to look up the differences between the two to make sure I was understanding the whole message God was giving me.

Scavenger Hunt: collecting clues to create a bigger picture.

Treasure Hunt: going after the "one thing" or treasure.

It's been a season where God has been taking me from a lack and an orphan mindset to the identity of being His daughter and a sonship mindset. I will say God knows how to speak to His kids in a way they will understand. I thought this analogy was so perfect for me for all those years of trying to figure it out and find the "pieces," the clues, that point to who I am in God. I have written everything down in hopes it points to some big calling or future. Grasping at any and all encouragement, subconsciously thinking, how does this fill me up so I can feel less insecure as a person?

However, what stood out to me was the treasure is going after the "one thing," every word I've received, dreams I've dreamed, and things He has been speaking to me, knowing that one thing is God. The "scavenger mindset" I was in was fueled by the fear of not finding all the right "clues" and missing out on what God had for me, or worse, missing where He was leading me. I was on the outside, finding a way "in."

With the "treasure mindset," I already have the map in my hands. God gave me the Holy Spirit to help navigate. This mindset is trusting in God to lead the way. He will light up the next step. Trusting that, "I know the plans I have for you, says the Lord. They are plans for good and not for disaster, to give you a future and a hope" (Jeremiah 29:11 NLT).

There is rest knowing that I don't have to strive because I know I am His daughter, and He is a good Father. He was reminding me that I no longer am scavenging like I don't know the truth, for I do, and He is leading the way.

Do you remember the movie, *The Lion King?* Remember the scene where Simba follows Rafiki to the water? He looks in the water, disappointed at his own reflection, because he was hoping to see his father. Simba thought his father was still alive. Then, as he looks a second time, he sees his own reflection turn into the reflection of his father *in* him, and his father appears in the sky. Mufasa, Simba's father, says something so profound.

Mufasa: Simba, you have forgotten me?

Simba: No! How could I?

Mufasa: You have forgotten who you are and so you have forgotten me…Remember who you are, YOU ARE MY SON.

#mindblown

If you want to learn to Stand in the Knowing of who God says you are, you have to start by believing and knowing you are a child of God. Everything else flows from knowing that truth. And that truth gets inside of us when we listen, receive, and respond to what God is speaking to us. *You have forgotten who you are and so you have forgotten **Me.*** When you don't know who you are, you have taken your eyes off of *Him*. When our world seems to be falling apart, God takes us left when we were expecting right. We must remember who He is and continue to keep our eyes on Him because that's how we remember *who we are,* daughters of the King!

Will you believe that God is who He says He is? Will you believe you are who He says you are? Will you allow healing when you think thoughts like, "I'm not enough; this is too big for me," or "I'm not qualified"? Will you run to Him instead of running away? God loves to remind you of who you are by showing you who He is.

I get it, it hits different when you're the one who has to make the choice to either let fear cripple you or take control of your life. Following Jesus into the unknown and trusting Him when He says it will be okay is scary, especially when it doesn't look or feel that way. Do it anyway! Take His hand despite it all. Continue to take those steps and remind yourself that you are a daughter of God and that He turns all things around for your good. Stand in the Knowing of who you are and whose you are by keeping your eyes on Him.

Friend, your dream, your "destination," was never about you. It was always about God *in* you.

Having Done All, Stand...

So, what does it mean to Stand in the Knowing?

It's not about clearing the gunk out of our lives so Jesus can pour more into us and activate our sonship. We already have His love. He has done it all—given us His name, His precious promises, His power to rule and reign in life. He wants to clear out the gunk so we can live for Him through eyes of love, purity, and wholeness; so we can operate in right standing without man-made filters and discern the enemy who tries to take our thoughts captive. It's about knowing God has done it all so that we can stand in the knowing that He will bring heaven down through us because of Him *in* us, to live in true freedom as a child of God.

Our calling is to keep our heads on His chest hearing Him breathe and our hearts sync. Being so close, we go where He goes and say what He says. You cannot step out of His timing when you live surrendered like this. If you walk away with one thing from this book, it would be that your heart burns to walk step-by-step with the Lord and follow Him wherever He leads you, out of love and not ahead of Him in worry and fear of missing it. You already **are** who God says you are. Embrace the journey as He walks with you in discovering your identity. Be honest, be vulnerable as you follow Him into the unknown of you. And, above all, continue to Stand in the Knowing that you are His masterpiece, created new in Christ Jesus, to do the good things He planned for you (ref. Ephesians 2:10 NLT).

ABOUT THE AUTHOR

 Wisconsin-raised musician and worship leader Anna Bachmeyer has been singing since she could talk. Her conversations with Jesus are filled with moments of spontaneous song and have inspired her to write from her heart. Her home life is filled with three rambunctious young boys and a dedicated husband, and they love spending time together, celebrating one another.

Anna's debut album, Kingdom Inside, can be found on all streaming platforms.

FOLLOW ANNA

Instagram, Facebook, YouTube: @theannabachmeyer
TikTok: @annabachmeyer.

If you enjoyed this book, I'd be so grateful if you'd
WRITE A REVIEW....

It's easy and helps my book get into the hands of more readers.
- Step 1: Go to www.AMAZON.com
- Step 2: Search for my book in Amazon books
- Step 3: Scroll down to REVIEWS
- Step 4: Leave a Review

I'd love to know your thoughts about my book. Contact me & let me know what you got out of the book.

Join my newsletter for more info on events and releases.

Sign up here: www.annabachmeyer.com.

Thank You for Your Support.

MORE FROM
ANNA BACHMEYER

Kingdom Inside
ANNA BACHMEYER

It started out with prophecy, *"There is a kingdom inside of you"*.

From the depths of a painful season with many things being stripped away and feeling laid bare, Anna took that prophetic word, along with her doubts, questions, confusion, and pain to God. These songs were written from the journey she went on to discover how God sees her, and how the revelation of those truths led her to step into her authentic identity in Him.

As you listen, her hope is that these songs would inspire and urge you to seek God with all of your heart, to go on your own unique journey with Him to discover who He says you are. There is a kingdom inside of you too. It's time for it to come out.

To listen and purchase, visit www.annabachmeyer.com.

At Square Tree Publishing, we believe your message matters. That is why our dedicated team of professionals is committed to bringing your literary texts and targeted curriculum to a global marketplace. We strive to make that message of the highest quality, while still maintaining your voice.

We believe in you, therefore, we provide a platform through website design, blogs, and social media campaigns to showcase your unique message. Our innovative team offers a full range of services from editing to graphic design inspired with an eye for excellence, so that your message is clearly and distinctly heard.

Whether you are a new writer needing guidance with each step of the process, or a seasoned writer, we will propel you to the next level of your development.

At Square Tree Publishing, it's all about launching YOU!

Apply TODAY to become a Square Tree author.
Go to www.squaretreepublishing.com
Click the **APPLY NOW** button.

Made in the USA
Monee, IL
25 June 2024

60631327R00098